MAIL JUMPER!

Elaine Kanelos

The Story of the First Mail Girl

ARCHWAY
PUBLISHING

Archway Publishing books may be ordered through booksellers or by contacting:

Archway Publishing
1663 Liberty Drive
Bloomington, IN 47403
www.archwaypublishing.com
1-(888)-242-5904

Because of the dynamic nature of the Internet, any web addresses or
links contained in this book may have changed since publication and
may no longer be valid. The views expressed in this work are solely those
of the author and do not necessarily reflect the views of the publisher,
and the publisher hereby disclaims any responsibility for them.

Any people depicted in stock imagery provided by Thinkstock are models,
and such images are being used for illustrative purposes only.
Certain stock imagery © Thinkstock.

ISBN: 978-1-4808-0751-8 (sc)
ISBN: 978-1-4808-0752-5 (e)

Library of Congress Control Number: 2014939811

Printed in the United States of America

Archway Publishing rev. date: 05/21/2014

Acknowledgements

I owe Harold Friestad, the life blood of Lake Geneva Cruise Line, a great debt. He was a wonderful first boss so many years ago, and now has patiently, and reliably, provided me with many of the details included in this book about the *Walworth*, *Walworth II*, and how the US Mail Boat tour has expanded and changed over time.

I must also thank my mother, Alice Kanelos, who dug through dusty files to find many details on each of our homes, and their history, for me. And who, along with my sisters Alexa and Jorjanne, endured my insistence that we go through hundreds of family slides to find photos from our childhood on the lake.

Finally, to Lake Geneva Cruise Line and Gage Marine for use of photos from my mail jumping days, and of the US Mail Boats.

Thank you all.

Contents

Before Mail Girls

*L*ake Geneva, Wisconsin, has been a favorite summer retreat of Chicago's rich and famous since the end of the Civil War when the city's wealthy—desiring to get away from the heat, germs, and congestion of urban Chicago—began frequenting the lake's beautiful shoreline.

From the 1870s through the turn of the twentieth century, the Gilded Age reigned in the United States, led by the first generation of Americans who were true urban magnates. Despite their enormous wealth, these men and their families were not completely insulated from cities' negative aspects, which included crime and pollution, as well as the illnesses, and diseases that were easily spread by under-developed sanitation systems. Summers were usually the worst time of the year in any city, and Chicago was no exception.

Chicago was officially only thirty-seven years old when the Gilded Age was ushered in, but it was already a booming industrial engine, and the fastest growing city in America. As it expanded, the city's wealthy began looking for places to take refuge from the city during the summer. Then, in 1871, the Great Chicago Fire destroyed the central business district as well as many of the social, and business, haunts of its newly-minted millionaires—the men fueling Chicago's economic boom.

Certainly the fire, and Chicago's destroyed downtown, added to its patriarchs' desire to seek summertime refuge for their families at countryside properties and second homes.

The summer estate boom in Lake Geneva, which began in the late 1800s, was also driven by the idealization of the English country house. It had come to the attention of America's growing class of millionaires that the English gentry often owned both a London house and a countryside estate to which they retreated in the summers. This combination of residences allowed them to enjoy the best of both country and city living. Moreover, these English families represented many generations of wealth passed down from parent to child, sometimes for hundreds of years. Chicago's newly-wealthy intended to create similar dynasties for their children and grandchildren; therefore, building country homes that could be passed down to future generations held an extra appeal.

Also during this period, society developed a distinct nostalgia for nature. Romanticism, which developed in Europe in the late eighteenth century, arrived in the United States at the turn of the twentieth. Partially a revolt against what industrialization was doing to cities, and the quality of life for its residents, Romanticism elevated the importance of nature. It helped spawn the Chautauqua Movement which promoted large family gatherings in natural settings for learning and cultural entertainment. The Arts and Crafts style became popular at the same time. Its influence idealized natural forms and emphasized craftsmanship in architecture, interior design, and the decorative arts.

All these influences contributed to Lake Geneva becoming

the summer home of Chicago's wealthy, and the building of spectacular, carefully-crafted estates along its shoreline. The area was close enough to the city to be accessible, yet nature was unsullied here, and the lake was a perfect gem around which to celebrate the beauty of summer.

Lake Geneva was a natural paradise. It was also malleable. The communities around the lake were barely settled. They were in the early adolescence of development, which allowed them to be molded around the influences of Chicago's wealthiest families.

Therefore, as is often the case, a unique combination of influences came together at just the right moment to create the Lake Geneva that we know today. What started in the 1870s continues today. Although Maple Lawn, the first mansion built on the lake, no longer stands; the lake remains a magnet for Chicago's wealthy and a much-loved vacation destination for other Midwesterners—whether they are here for a day, a weekend, or longer.

From the beginning, the families who built mansions on the lake found themselves isolated from more than just the negative aspects of city summers. Their summer sojourns were several months long. Usually the family, often including extended family members, would relocate to their Lake Geneva home for the entire summer. Children, in-laws, siblings with their families, and servants, all moved en masse. For the majority of the family, there was little, if any, travel back and forth to Chicago once they had arrived. Only the patriarch would move between the lake and city with any regularity.

Telephone lines were not installed until 1875, and service was spotty for many years afterwards. For all of these reasons, families wanted and needed, their mail. Mail and newspapers were the main portals of communication. The arrival of the *Chicago Tribune* or the *Chicago Daily News* enabled families on summer retreat to catch up with happenings in the city. Their connection to family members who were not with them, the goings-on in society during their absence, and the news of the day all flowed through the US mail.

If you owned a mansion on the shoreline of Lake Geneva, there was only one truly dependable way to get the mail: by water. There were good reasons for this. Roads around the lake were narrow and unpaved. They were often far from the estate's main house. In addition, much of the property around the lake was boggy, and, as time passed, more and more lakeside homes included significant estates. As a result, public roads ended at the estate gates—which were often a mile or more from the estate house.

The lake has a twenty-one-mile shoreline that undulates in and out of large bays and rises to several high points. Most roads are set back a significant distance from the shoreline; therefore, it would have taken a mailman on horseback, or in a buggy, more than a full day to deliver the mail to all the towns and estates on the lake using the available land routes. Delivery by boat was much faster and more direct.

Lake Geneva is seven and a half miles long, two miles wide at its widest point, and only a half mile across at its narrowest section. Even today, the fastest route from one lakeshore location to another is very often by boat. In summer, residents have always used the water as a main thoroughfare; whether traveling to a friend's home, into town, or to pick up visitors from the train depots that once existed in several locations around the lake.

In 1874, three years after the Sturgis family built Maple Lawn, the first steamboat was launched on the lake. A variety of marine delivery services began shortly after steam arrived. In 1894, the

Chicago Daily Tribune referenced paper delivery on the lake via the steamboat *Wilbur F,* and in the late 1800s, the *Cornelian* was delivering dairy items to homes along the lakeshore.

In 1916, mail delivery started in earnest on the lake, and mail has been delivered via boat continuously during summers ever since. Only two boats have ever had the honor of being called the US Mail Boat on Lake Geneva, and it wasn't until fifty-eight years later, in 1974, that a girl was hired to deliver the mail by jumping on and off of a moving boat full of spectators—come rain or shine.

I was that girl. And this is a story of growing up on Lake Geneva, breaking traditions in order to make a childhood dream come true, and creating a new tradition—one in which women are always a part of the team that jumps the mail on Lake Geneva.

Summer Girl

My story about becoming Lake Geneva's first Mail Girl can't be properly told without sharing my experiences growing up there. Living on Lake Geneva—interacting with the mansions, the people, and the water—shaped my life, my views, and my personality. So that is where I will start.

At first I was a Summer Girl.

There is a difference in Lake Geneva. You can be a summer person, a local, or a tourist. Eventually, at different times in my life, I would be all three.

The locals and the summer residents may mingle. They may become friends, they may end up changing into either a local or a summer person—they may even marry one another. Or, like me, they may end up as a tourist—a visitor passing through for a day, or week of vacation, or to see old friends.

But the designation, whichever applies to you, is part life in Lake Geneva. As in, "She lives on the lake, but she's a local." Or, "He's a lifeguard at the Williams Bay beach, and he's a summer guy."

These designations aren't better or worse than each other, they are just identifiers, and somehow they work. But it's important to note that you can only be one of these designations at any one time. You are one, or you are another. Nothing else is possible.

WESTGATE AND FISHING LURES

For the first twenty-three years of my life, summertime meant Lake Geneva. The first place we lived on the lake was a summer apartment my parents rented at Westgate, one of the many lakefront mansions built in the early twentieth century.

In 1917, Gertrude Allen was a twenty-seven-year-old, single, young woman who had recently inherited a fortune. Her grandfather had built a tannery in Kenosha, Wisconsin, decades before, and her father and uncle had expanded the family business. In the 1860s, their business grew exponentially due to a high demand for leather goods during the Civil War, and a family fortune was made.

When her father died unexpectedly in 1911, he left Gertrude and her two brothers each with sizable inheritances. One of Gertrude's first moves was to purchase land on Lake Geneva and hire English architect Clement Brun to design an English Manor-style home. Construction began in 1917.

At the same time that Gertrude was building Westgate, my extended family began sinking roots in Lake Geneva. My great grandmother's brother, Jesse Parker Shannon, moved to Lake Geneva from Belvedere, Illinois, in about 1910.

Jesse was an entrepreneur, albeit on a much smaller scale than the Chicago scions whose mansions dotted the area. He started by building a hotel in the town of Lake Geneva for weekend visitors. The building still stands—today as a somewhat downtrodden, unoccupied structure on Broad Street just across from Horticulture Hall.

An avid fisherman, Jesse's true calling was as the inventor of several fishing lures. His most famous was the *Shannon Twin Spinner*, a bass lure that he designed at the lake in 1915 and patented in 1927. The *Shannon Twin Spinner* is considered by many to be the most effective bass lure ever. It spawned most of the modern spinners used in bass fishing today. As recently as 2012, the *Shannon Twin Spinner* was featured in *Field and Stream Magazine*, which pronounced it, "the predecessor of all modern spinner baits." Jesse went on to develop several other lures with such memorable names as the *Shannon Porker* and the *Shannon Weed Master*. So, my family connection to the lake started at about the same time that Gertrude was planning her life in Lake Geneva.

While Gertrude's English country house was being built, she married George Westgate. Then tragedy struck. While visiting family in New York, Gertrude, pregnant with their first child, was swept up in an influenza epidemic that killed thousands, including Gertrude. She died in 1918 at the age of twenty-eight.

George inherited Gertrude's fortune and saw Westgate completed in the early 1920s. Built of hand-hewn granite blocks, the exterior walls were two feet thick, the living room featured a pink granite fireplace, and the basement contained a bowling alley. It was the essence of the English country house that America's wealthy so wanted to own. George Westgate lived there in the summers until 1940, when he sold the estate.

By the time my parents rented at Westgate in the mid-1950s, the house had been divided into apartments. Ours consisted of several rooms on the west end of the second story, in what had originally been the children's wing.

My best friend at Westgate was Ann Herring. Her family lived in what had originally been the estate's carriage house. The building had later been converted into a nine-car garage and caretaker house, and by the time we were summering at Westgate, the carriage house had been repurposed again, this time to the Herring's home. They were our closest neighbors, and I remember Ann and I—as precocious four, five, and six year olds—spending our days on the acres of lawns, safely restricted by the estate's thick granite wall.

We didn't get our mail by boat at Westgate. Marine delivery on the lake is only available to houses with a Lake Geneva post office address. If your mailing address is Fontana or Williams Bay, marine delivery is not available. Home owners can, however, establish a Lake Geneva P.O. Box and receive mail by marine delivery that way. Despite not getting our mail via the Mail Boat in those days, I saw the boat go by daily while we played on the front lawn.

Westgate was razed in 2008, but the original granite wall that enclosed the estate can still be seen as you drive along South Lake Shore Drive just east of Abbey Springs Yacht Club. The carriage house still stands, continuing its life as a private residence.

A New House and New Antics

My seventh summer, we moved to our own summer house at 668 South Lake Shore Drive. The 1960s-style house had one level, an abundance of glass on the lake side, and four bedrooms. Three were occupied by my parents, my older sister, Jorjanne, and my little brother, Andrew. The fourth room I shared with my younger sister, Alexa.

Whether at Lake Geneva or in River Forest, Illinois, where we lived the rest of the year, Alexa and I shared a bedroom for our entire lives, right up until the day she got married. As a result, we became life-long partners in crime. During the next six summers, while we lived on the south shore, Alexa and I ran rampant across the lawn, down the creek, through the fields, and into the lake every day, all day, from Memorial Day until Labor Day.

Unlike Westgate, which sat on an eastward-sloping hillside that rose from the lakeshore, this house sat in the lowlands that mark the Narrows on both the south and north shores. This narrowest part of the lake is less than half a mile across, and on calm summer nights you can hear conversations on the other shore as clearly as if those speaking were sitting right beside you.

This lawn was flat and broad with two small saplings and one mature birch tree in the front yard, along with two wide, sand beaches at the shoreline that were separated by a narrow lane of grass leading to our pier. The pier, like most on the lake, was about ten feet wide along the central spine and narrower—maybe three feet wide—where it branched out to form boat slips.

My parents owned a Gage-Hacker, a boat designed specifically to cut gracefully through the often choppy waters on Lake Geneva. Russell Gage, the founder of Gage Marine and the Lake Geneva Cruise Line, which runs the Mail Boat and other excursion boats on the lake, worked with his son Bill, and John L. Hacker, to develop a beautiful, smooth-riding boat. Its clean lines and high quality mahogany craftsmanship were designed for beauty, speed, and an ability to perform in any kind of weather.

Our Gage-Hacker was twenty-six-feet long with a beam of just over eight feet and a twenty-four-inch draft. The engine was a three-hundred-horsepower V-8. Gage-Hackers were only produced for six years, between 1961 and 1967, which quickly made them iconic and highly sought-after on the lake.

We also had a Sunfish sailboat and a fifteen-foot Boston Whaler, both of which were easily deployed off of the boat dock located just in front of one of the sand beaches.

During the years we summered at that house, my sisters, brother, and I climbed into the Gage-Hacker for Friday night rides to fish fry dinners at lakeside restaurants, to learn to water ski, or when the family was headed to a barbeque at friends' houses across the lake.

The Baumbachs were my parents' best friends. Their summer home was across the lake on the very tip of Cedar Point. The house was built in 1929 by the first Emil A. Baumbach, the owner of a Chicago tool and die business. Just as we were a family primarily of girls, they were a family primarily of boys. Mark, Chris, and Emil were almost perfectly matched in age to Alexa, Andrew, and me, and we saw them constantly. A trip to the Baumbach house was forty-five minutes in the car, but only fifteen by boat.

Although I was occasionally grossed out by the boys' obsession with frogs and insects (I preferred toads), I was deeply intrigued by their prowess with Black Cat firecrackers, and fishing abilities. One of our many shared family events was the annual Hobo Party. The Baumbach clan arrived by boat, of course. The three boys sporting ragged shorts and tee shirts, charcoal beards, and polka dot bandanas on sticks. Uncle Emil was always similarly attired, with the addition of his ever-present cigar, which for this occasion was smoked down to the nub. Only my Aunt Lynn arrived with any semblance of respectability. Dinner was always hot dogs and baked beans.

Another annual boat event was the Fourth of July fireworks display over Fontana Beach. Along with hundreds of other families, we cruised down the lake to watch from the boat as fireworks exploded over the beach. Several years later, I would get my "boat wings" and permission to drive our boats. But those are tales for a later chapter.

Fields and Crawfish

For me, and all the children in our little neighborhood group, on any, and every, sunny day the pier was Ground Central. Most days we spent entirely on the pier from early morning until sunset. We might wander off to other activities for hours at a time, but eventually, we always ended up back on the pier for a last swim, to watch a storm marching across the lake, or because we'd been ordered there to pick up the fishing poles, minnow nets, masks, fins, towels, buckets of fish, cans of worms, and half-eaten mid-day snacks that littered its broad white planks.

From the sand beaches, we had immediate access to the water as well. We waded into the clear, spring-fed lake for crawfish hunts, or to collect lake rocks, seaweed, and snail shells. In the sand, we caught white and yellow butterflies, created castles, dug holes, and occasionally lost important things our parents had told us not to bury there.

In the back yard, there were a dozen big maples and oaks. My dad hung a tree swing from the branch of one, and two others served as cross ties for our horses, which shared the hundred-acre field behind the house with Mr. Massey's herd of cows. We were too young to ride the horses, so Alexa and I spent endless hours crisscrossing the field in search of adventures, or using it as a short cut to the small neighborhood store on Linn Road. Because we were barefoot nearly all the time, the trip through the field could be particularly precarious, studded as it was with thistles and cow pies.

To the east of our house was the Kinzer's house. Their property was fascinating because a stream ran from the hundred-acre field to the lake through their yard, and ended in a boggy pond just before merging with the lake. There were tadpoles, frogs, and water-skimmers to be had in that stream, and we found the algae-covered pond fascinating. We really couldn't keep ourselves out of either of them.

To the west, our immediate neighbors, the Severins, had three grandchildren our age, and a magical, child-sized car made by Grandpa Severin, and named the Putt-Putt. The Putt-Putt had a wood chasse attached to a go-cart base. There were no doors or roof, just four-on-the-floor, a steering wheel, room for two in the body, and jump-seat on the back that doubled as a trunk. It was red.

If you were some age older than I ever was, you could drive the Putt-Putt. The rest of us were just happy to get rides. Pretending to be on our way out to dinner, Alexa and I pulled fancy white taffeta slips over our bathing suits and bumped along in the Putt-Putt as we were driven all over the Severin's yard.

Just past the Severin's was the log-cabin summer home of Illinois State Senator Arthur J. Bidwell, whose hoard of grandchildren (two handfuls of boys and one girl) were summer people as well. This motley assembly, in some form or another, was our summer neighborhood gang. We moved like a frenetic school of minnows across yards, in and out of the water, down the stream, and into the field day-in and day-out.

Every day at about three, we congregated at my house for a very important daily treat: ice cream.

My father and his three sisters were second generation owners of Andes Candies, started by my grandfather in Chicago in 1921. Beginning with a single store selling hand-dipped chocolates, my grandfather—whom we called Papou—expanded Andes to more than one hundred locations in Chicago, and nearby suburbs, over the next thirty years.

I remember going with my father to the "Kitchen," the area

at the company headquarters and production plant in downtown Chicago where the hand-dipped chocolates were made. The rest of the plant was much like any manufacturing area and the offices were no different from other offices, but the Kitchen was special. It was carefully protected by doors that were always carefully sealed to keep the Kitchen pristine and sanitary. Large windows looked into the Kitchen from the plant, letting us see in without disturbing the chocolate-making going on inside.

Any time I was allowed to go into the Kitchen, I was always on my best behavior. Despite the big stoves that were always warming chocolate or nougat in two-foot wide copper kettles set on the gas flames, the room was always chilly. It was kept at a low temperature to keep the completed, hand-dipped chocolates cool.

My Papou died when I was four years old, and my father took over as President of Andes.

The summer we moved to 668, my dad had a special ice cream freezer delivered to the house. It held three, five-gallon drums of chocolate and vanilla Andes ice cream. Regular deliveries arrived throughout the summer, and periodically a carton of three hundred sugar cones arrived as well, which was why every day at three, our gaggle of kids would stream across the lawn to the ice cream freezer where my mom served up triple and quadruple scoops piled on sugar cones for everyone. When we finished, sticky chocolate and vanilla rivulets had run down our arms and legs—a problem easily solved by a jump in the lake.

Mail Boys and Tadpoles

Like all the other summer residents, as a Summer Girl, I arrived at the lake the first weekend after the school year ended, and left a day or two before school started again after Labor Day.

Between those two dates, I only put shoes on to go to fish fry dinners, or for the two or three trips we made into town.

My friends all belonged to other summer families. We spent every day for the entire summer together and then we went back to wherever it was we had come from—and we didn't see, talk to, or even think about one another until summer came again.

Likewise, during the summer, I had no connection with my "other" life—school, winter, or city friends. The only flimsy connection to that world was the *Weekly Reader* school magazine that arrived by Mail Boat every Thursday. It was my only reminder that somewhere in the ether, my other world was going on without me.

Similar to many of the other summer residents on the lake, we didn't have a "land" mailbox, we only had the mailbox nailed to the pier post. In the eyes of the US Post Office, our only address was Pier 668.

The Mail Boat and the Mail Jumper were already legends to me and my friends. The Mail Boat came every day. The second that one of us spotted it, or heard its horn blow, all action stopped. The Mail Boat arrived at our pier at 11:40 a.m., and because, year after year, the captain tries to stay on schedule, its arrival was a fairly reliable vehicle by which to plan the day.

In those days, the Mail Boat was not the *Walworth II* that I jumped the mail from, and on which the mail is still delivered today. It was the original *Walworth,* named after the county in which the lake and all its shore towns are located.

The original *Walworth* was built in 1916 for sightseeing on the lake, and became the first Mail Boat when water delivery officially started that same year.

A seventy-four foot steamship, she had an elegantly bowed hull, narrow beam, and a deck that was low to the waterline—similar to many of the other Lake Geneva steamships of the era. By the time she was delivering mail to my pier on the south shore, the *Walworth* had been converted to a gasoline engine and had been carrying passengers and mail around the lake for nearly fifty years.

On our stretch of the south shore, mail was delivered to four piers in a row. Arriving from the west, the first jump was at the Bidwell's pier, then the Severin's, followed by our pier, and finally the Kinzer's. Past the Kinzer's pier, the *Walworth* followed the shoreline past the mouth of the Kinzer's stream and the Linn Road municipal pier before making more mail deliveries at the Seven Hundred Club.

At our low point on the lake, the Mail Boat and Mail Jumper were visible for the entire four pier series and we wanted to see every bit of action. On any given day, our gang of children rushed out onto whichever pier we were closest to, in order to have the best possible view of the brave Mail Boy risking it all by jumping off the fast-moving *Walworth*.

By the time the Mail Boat reached our part of the lake, we had been in the water for hours. But toast-brown and sopping wet, we stopped everything for those few minutes to soak in every detail of the day's delivery.

Sometimes, one of us would stand at the very tip of the pier and hold out a hand so that the Mail Boy could lean out, with one knee hitched over the *Walworth's* mahogany handrail, and hand us the mail. That was daring on our part, but it didn't happen very often. We all preferred to watch him jump. Seeing the Mail Boy jump off of the moving boat packed full of wide-eyed passengers was the pinnacle—the best of everything.

It was the sun, the water, the captain telling his tales of the lake over the boat's PA system, the tourists, the speed, and the Mail Jumper. It was magic.

First, there was the approach. The boat came incredibly close to the pier, but still far enough away that the Mail Boy had to leap across six to eight feet of water to reach the pier. The Mail Boat never stopped—that was the amazing thing about it! And since it wasn't stopping, it came at us much faster than any other boat would ever approach a pier. Mail in hand, the Jumper climbed entirely out of the boat and stood on the narrow rub rail. His sneakers barely fit on the narrow ledge. He held the mail in his right hand, and used his left to grasp the edge of the boat's canopy.

His eyes were focused. You could see him planning. Getting ready. Deciding on the right moment, the split-second when he had the best chance at success.

Then came the jump. It was always so fast. He was on the pier. He was at the box. The mailbox door was open. The mail was in the box. The mailbox door slammed shut. He spun, took a few steps, then, with a leap, he was back on the still-speeding boat.

And then they were gone.

It was all so fast, so spectacular. We didn't want to move. We didn't want to breathe. We certainly didn't want to blink. Blink and you missed it.

Our mailbox was nailed to the second-to-last post on the narrow, left side of the second boat slip. This made delivery at our pier more harrowing than most. First, that section of pier was quite narrow. But second, because of the way the shoreline curved, the *Walworth* had to approach at an angle—with the bow aimed out—instead of being able to slip by parallel to the pier, as was ideal. This meant less boat-side access to the pier and a curved, backward jump for the Mail Boy.

As far as we were concerned, this was clearly a precision jump. No room for error here. Maybe we heard this from our parents, but we believed that we had one of the harder jumps on the Mail Boat route, and we didn't want to be absent, or otherwise engaged, when the Mail Boy finally missed and went in the drink right at our house.

This never happened, of course, but not for want of trying on our part. As the years passed, we spent hours devising ways to foil the Mail Boys' incredible luck. Several times a summer, we poured buckets of water on the mailbox portion of the pier minutes before the *Walworth* arrived. We tried yelling and screaming to distract the Jumper. We put all manner of nasty things—dead fish and dried up crabs—in the mailbox to disorient him. We even threatened to soap down the pier, but someone's parent always intervened before we could actually try it.

It was a magical few seconds, seven days a week, for one hundred days of our year. Any day that there was no mail for us was a bad day. Not because we wanted mail, but because, if there wasn't mail to deliver, the *Walworth* would zip by thirty or forty feet out from the end of the pier. All we'd get was an occasional wave from the Mail Jumper, the captain, or the tourists.

Watching the Mail Boy make the jumps was a major daily event. Day after day, year after year, all summer long, and it was always thrilling. We never got tired of waiting for the Mail Boy.

FRONT DOORS AND LAKE HIKES

There are many traditions on Lake Geneva, the Mail Jumper being one of them. But others are worth noting too. One is that the "front" of every house on the lake is considered to be on the lakeside. This creates an interesting issue because everyone's front door is, therefore, on the back of the house. I had great fun confusing city visitors with instructions to go in the front door at the back of the house, or to meet me on the front lawn, which to them seemed to be the backyard and the backyard the front yard.

Another tradition is hiking around the lake. As far back as the days of the Potawatomie tribe, who originally settled the lake, a trail existed along the water's edge. Over time, the majority of property owners, somewhat by mutual agreement, left the few feet adjacent to the shoreline accessible for anyone to walk along and enjoy the lake. In the 1970s, the public right of way became law, but for many years before and since, hiking around the lake has been a rite of passage for the kids growing up on it.

My first hike was when I was about eight. I went under the care of my older sister, but didn't make it all the way. I recall being picked up in Williams Bay, just a little more than half way around; but in reality, I may only have made it a quarter of the way to the town of Lake Geneva.

The next year I tried again with two friends. In those days of no cell phones or neoprene sportswear, we left pre-dawn and knew we had to push hard to make it home before dark. Our mothers supplied us with peanut butter and jelly sandwiches, Girl Scout canteens full of soon-to-be lukewarm Kool-Aid, and dimes so that we could report in from payphones in Lake Geneva, Williams Bay, and Fontana.

Additional stops were made at the houses of family friends— and these were always the best. Announcing the date of your hike was a big deal. On hike day, your friends were on the lookout for your bedraggled arrival; worrying if you were running late, and impressed if you got to their house earlier than they had planned. Their mothers were on the ready with Band Aids, food, water, bathrooms, and dry socks or shorts. There were plenty of questions too. "How did you make it around Turtle Pond?" "Did you have to go in the lake to get around the fence that someone had built right to the water's edge?" "How many blisters do you have?"

I made it all the way around the lake that year—and the next, and the next. Eventually, I became an old pro at hiking the lake's twenty-one miles. I learned to wear a swim suit under my shorts so that I could take a swim to cool off and not have to wear soaked cotton shorts for the rest of the hike. I learned to bring water, not Kool-Aid, extra socks, and sunscreen, and to buy lunch at a town stop instead of packing my own.

The summer I was eleven, Mark Baumbach, along with a pack of boys from Cedar Point Park, ran around the lake. They got home so early that they went around again that same day. Our house was their halfway point, which meant that they came running up our front lawn at about ten in the morning and then again at around four o'clock that afternoon.

I never really got over that feat. It was too impressive.

Having already made my hike a few weeks earlier, I called it a wrap. Even though I used the lake path frequently throughout high school and college as a shorter route to friends' houses, or just to enjoy walking along the shoreline, I never hiked around the lake again.

DRY DOCK AND BOAT CUSHIONS

Gage Marine and the Lake Geneva Cruise Line have been owned by the Gage family since 1958, and my family was a loyal customer from the start. At some point during nearly every weekend, there was a trip to Gage Marine in Williams Bay. My dad held lengthy discussions about our boats with Russell and Bill Gage, and then loaded up on boating essentials such as gas, safety cushions, and marine flashlights.

Even in the winter, when we went to snowmobile and ice skate on the lake, the weekend always included a trip to the Gage

Marine dry dock barns. I liked going to Gage, but the trips often lasted longer than my attention span.

While my dad talked boats, I led Alexa and Andrew on explorations of everywhere we were not supposed to go in the boatyard. We wandered underneath half-painted, thousand-pound hulls, and climbed up ladders leaned against boats, then hiked head-first into their cabins to check out the newly installed upholstery and teak decking. We browsed the supply store, untwisting the first six feet of yellow marine rope wrapped around giant dowels, and setting off all of the chimes on the boat clocks lined up for sale.

Years later, it would be Bill Gage that I would write to with my idea of becoming the first Mail Girl.

BLACK POINT AND HORSE BUBBLES

By the summer I was eleven, I had graduated from minnow nets to horses. Years of lessons had earned me the privilege of riding at the lake. As far as I was concerned, riding here was far better than at the stables in Oak Park where we kept our two geldings in the winter.

While my sisters came to love arena styles of riding—one became a nationally ranked competitor in hunter class jumping and the other studied dressage—I am the one who learned to cut cattle at round-ups in Wyoming, and galloped across the Great Rift Valley with a herd of Zebra aboard a Kenyan polo pony. That love of riding in wide-open spaces began on the rides that Joey Bidwell and I took through the fields behind the lake during my eleventh summer.

Joe's bay gelding had joined our grey hunter, Beau Chief, and palomino quarter horse, Larry, and—of course—the

Massey cows, in the hundred-acre field that summer. It became the summer of horses for me. Joe and I, who had grown up as summer friends, went off on day-long explorations several times a week. We would saddle up with a pack of sandwiches and chips and head off.

The road we lived on ended five houses to the west of the Bidwells. A two-by-six plank nailed crosswise to two trees marked the end of the road. Someone had made a half-hearted effort to paint yellow stripes across it. We would guide our horses easily around the barrier and then follow a narrow deer trail through the woods, emerging on country roads that led to open fields where we would ride, talk, and explore.

Usually, we ended up at Black Point, which was privately owned, but unfenced and mostly open woods. We made our way through the forest and would circle the Black Point lagoon in order to emerge onto a small, isolated sandy beach. There we'd eat lunch and let the horses wade into the lake to cool off and drink. Larry, always a bit of a smart-aleck, liked to play with the water more than drink it. He would toss his head sending sprays of water out onto the lake and then stick his nose in up to his eyes and blow bubbles. These are things that no self-respecting horse would ever do. But that was Larry.

My Summer Girl years were magical. Every day in the summer was an adventure in imagination, energy, and friends. We started early in the morning, and didn't quit until long after the last lightening bug had been caught and the mosquitos drove us indoors. Then we collapsed into bed, planning new adventures for the next day before sleep caught us mid-sentence. Every day was unique, and at the same time, exactly the same as the day before. They threaded together like a daisy-chain necklace—light, bright, and easy.

Then Labor Day arrived and the lake was gone. It was back to the city—to sidewalks, and schedules, and school friends. It was a completely different life, starting with the fact that we had to wear shoes.

The house I lived in at 668 South Lake Shore Drive, like Westgate, no longer exists. It was replaced in about 1990 by a much larger summer home. Access to the hundred-acre field is blocked by trees and undergrowth now, and the sand boxes are long gone; but the stream next door is still there, winding through the shade toward the lake.

Local Lake Girl

As with many of us, things changed for me in middle school. I started to see boys as more than just co-conspirators in the day's fun and games. It was also the year that I stopped being a Summer Girl.

For a few years, my dad had been transitioning Andes Candies away from retail. Andes had developed a very successful, bite-sized candy that sandwiched a layer of mint between two layers of chocolate. He decided to build the future of the company around wholesale distribution of the Andes Crème de Menthe. He was also ready to live in Lake Geneva year-round, so he began construction of new offices and a manufacturing facility in Delavan, Wisconsin, only ten miles to the west.

That summer, as in the past, within days of the school year ending, we packed up and headed to the lake. But this time, we would not be going back to the suburbs after Labor Day. We were moving to Lake Geneva year round. We were about to become locals.

Our new home was a stately, red-brick Georgian-style house

standing on a sloping hillside behind twenty-seven mature maples just west of the Narrows on the north shore.

The house was built in 1947 by Nathan B. Hunt, whose family started Hunt, Helm and Ferris Company in Harvard, Illinois, in 1916. Hunt, Helm and Ferris manufactured tools for farming. They patented and sold over two hundred and fifty products including a windmill, land roller, barbed wire stretcher and manure spreaders. Over the next fifty years, the company went through a series of mergers and acquisitions. In the 1980s, the company was bought by three private investors and renamed Starline Products. One of Starline's divisions, CannonBall:HNP, continued to operate in Harvard until 1991 when it moved to Beloit, Wisconsin.

Our new house was just two doors west of Alta Vista, one of the major estates on the lake. Alta Vista was designed in 1919 by Howard Van Doren Shaw, one of Chicago's best known architects. A Chicagoan by birth, Shaw graduated from Yale and then the Massachusetts Institute of Technology (MIT), one of the few schools in the US that had an architecture school. Returning to Chicago in 1891, he joined the architecture firm of Jenney and Mundie. His boss, William Le Baron Jenney, is credited with designing the first skyscraper, and in addition to Shaw, his firm employed Daniel Burnham and Louis Sullivan who would become key architects of the Chicago skyline.

Shaw designed several prominent commercial buildings in Chicago. He also designed private estates in Lake Forest, Illinois, and on Chicago's Gold Coast. During that same period, he designed Alta Vista and a few other significant homes on Lake Geneva.

Like most owners of larger shoreline properties, Nate Hunt had a caretaker, Ted Casper, who was responsible for keeping the property in top shape. In order to have his caretaker on the property at all times, in the 1950s Hunt added a two-story apartment onto the east side of the house for Ted and his family. The addition included a living room, dining room, two baths and two bedrooms. When we bought the house in 1968, Hunt moved to The Abbey Resort, keeping a boat and a condominium on the Abbey grounds for several years.

This house was very different from our house on the south shore. It was a year-round residence with a stately elegance and formality that was much more like our home in River Forest had been. There would be no climbing out the bedroom windows, or using the boat ladder to avail ourselves of the view from the roof at this house.

The house had five bedrooms, which were assigned exactly as they had been in previous homes, with Alexa and I sharing ours, which created a guest room for visitors. Our bedroom was longer than it was wide, with a pair of paned windows at opposite ends of the room. Each of us could lie in bed and look out over the front lawn and down onto the lake. The horses made the move with us and, during that first summer, the property was a buzz of activity as stables and a tennis court were built. Eventually a pool was added as well.

It was a summer of adjusting to new things. Being on the lake was the same, but just about everything else was different. One noticeable change for me was how differently the lake reflected light here. On the south shore, the gold, pink, and peach of every sunset is reflected against the surface of the lake to breathtaking effect. On the north shore, the sun sets behind you, so there are no sparkling sunsets; but moonlight paints a dramatic path across the lake at night.

Unlike our south shore home, where the house, lawn, and lake were all on the same level, this house was on a hillside. The shoreline was rocky and steep, with thick bushes clinging to the hillside as it plunged down to the water. We accessed the pier via a wide, twenty-step staircase, so there was no more wading into the lake from the shore. But the fact was, we'd outgrown our crawfish hunts.

The biggest change was that there was no neighborhood clan of friends. That first summer as year-round residents, I discovered that the vast majority of our new neighbors were older, or without children. On top of that, we lived on eleven acres, and behind us stretched many more acres of fields and woods, so we had a very limited number of neighbors. The days of running with a troop of kids were clearly over. I kept myself busy riding, learning to play tennis, and hanging out on the pier.

When autumn arrived, everyone who lived on either side of us for a dozen houses in each direction, including Alta Vista, packed up and went back to the city. We soon learned that life on the lake during the winter could be very isolated.

Addresses and Mailboxes

Our address, 88 North Lake Shore Drive, had nothing to do with its location on the street where the driveway entrance was located. Like most of the houses with an address of Lake Shore Drive on Lake Geneva, it is not technically on a road named Lake Shore Drive. In fact, there is no single road called Lake Shore Drive, instead there are a series of inter-connected roads that trace the shoreline, some named Lake Shore Drive, and others not. But if you have a house on the lake, your address is probably Lake Shore Drive, regardless of what street you actually live on.

The number of the address is assigned based roughly on the house's location on the lake. Although numbers start on the north shore as you leave the town of Lake Geneva and continue by lakefront lots along the water's edge, they don't follow a standard format. Eighty-eight might be located between eighty-seven and eighty-nine, or it might not be. And 668 might not be the 668th house on the lake. But it follows a rough order and progresses around the lake until you come back to the town of Lake Geneva.

Lakeshore addresses are further defined by adding either North or South. Our new house was on the north shore and fairly close to town, while 668 was on the south shore and about mid-way between Fontana and the town of Lake Geneva. Several year ago, the city of Lake Geneva changed their address system, but outside the city limits most houses still use the Lake Shore Drive designation.

Technically, our house was accessed via Snake Road. Snake Road is one of the more famous roads in the area. It has two entrances off of Highway 50. You'll find the first access to Snake Road at the bottom of the hill as you leave the town of Lake Geneva. Less than two miles further along the highway, it emerges again.

As its name implies, it winds for two and a half miles— through the woods, and up and down the hills—behind many of the lake's most famous historic estates. These homes were originally built on large tracts of land that supported barns, guest houses, greenhouses, caretaker cottages and other assorted estate buildings. Many of these historic estates still have all, or most, of their property intact, and most bear an estate name in addition to its address. Whatever time of year you make the trip, a drive down Snake Road is always beautiful. You will see the grand entrances to each estate, but you won't see the estate houses themselves. They are half a mile, or more, down private drives, which is why cruising the lake will always be the best way to see the wonderful homes on Lake Geneva and hear the history of each.

While our driveway was accessed from Snake Road, we didn't have a grand entrance. We had two spindly, white-picket-fence wings that had mostly collapsed under the weight of weeds and vines, and a driveway that was gravel from its start on Snake Road to about a thousand feet from the house, where it became blacktop. It was a mile long, and the "land" mailbox—which we only used in the winter when marine delivery wasn't available— was at the opposite end of the drive from the house.

Every fall and spring, rain and snowmelt washed out the driveway. This meant that we had to serpentine from one side of the narrow drive to the other at about four miles per hour to avoid getting stuck.

A Snake Road tradition is the use of "wood" in many of the estates names. Wychwood, Northwoodside, House in the Woods, and Edgewood are just a few of the estate names along Snake Road; so my mother decided that our house needed a name as well. She christened it Tanglewood, apropos of the unmanaged forest we had to drive through to get to Snake Road.

There was also a second way to exit Tanglewood. We could take a left turn about a quarter mile down the driveway from the house onto another narrow road. This side-road provided access to the five lakeshore houses to the west of us. It ended at Chapin Road, one of a handful of roads around the lake that run from one of the larger County roads directly to the water, and can be used as a boat launch.

In bad weather, the Chapin Road access route was significantly more reliable as a way to get to and from the house, but it wasn't really our driveway, and while we used it a great deal, the mailbox remained on Snake Road. This meant that if the weather was bad or the driveway impassable, we either went days without getting any mail, or we had to drive to the mailbox and then double back to Chapin Road in order to get home.

The entire process of getting mail and accessing the rest of humanity was much easier in the summer, when the lake was our highway and the mail was delivered to the pier. We could see the pier mailbox from nearly every room in the house—including my bedroom window—and it was an easy stroll across the front lawn and down the steps to retrieve it, which is the very reason that marine mail delivery has thrived on Lake Geneva for one hundred years.

Whalers and Paint Brushes

Our pier at this new house was longer and wider than the one on the south shore. There was the wood staircase leading to the pier, and in place of a boat dock for the sail boat and Whaler, my dad had installed Shore Stations on either side of the pier in the shallow water. There was one boat slip which faced at a right angle to the main pier, and the narrow arm of the slip was on the shore side. Our mailbox was mounted on a post that stood squarely in the middle of a twenty-by-twenty-foot sun-bathing deck at the end of the pier. One thing was for certain, based on its layout, instead of having one of the hardest piers on the lake for the Mail Jumper to jump, we now had one of the easiest.

This was the summer that I was first allowed to drive the Whaler, and it marked a new freedom. Boston Whalers are considered by many to be among the safest boats. They're unsinkable, untippable, and pretty hard to destroy. Therefore, our thirteen-foot Whaler, with its thirty-three horsepower outboard motor on the back, was a perfect kid's boat.

I was free to race around the lake at will. There were trips to Turtle Pond on the south shore, impromptu visits to the Baumbachs, and to the piers of other friends along the lakeshore. Occasionally, I would tie up at the municipal piers in either Williams Bay or Fontana to buy snacks, or just see what was up. Often, I took the Whaler out simply for a joy ride. There was nothing quite like gunning the outboard motor to its max and letting my hair whip out behind me as the Whaler's flat hull skipped across the top of the waves.

There is another Lake Geneva tradition that I should mention. Every pier on the lake is painted white—only white. Occasionally you might see one with the posts painted green or with a single red stripe painted around the top of the posts. Both of these variations may be, I believe, for safety's sake. Also, some of the commercial piers—the Riviera pier ("the Riv") for example—are not painted. They're too large, and the commercial traffic makes it unmanageable to keep the paint looking crisp. But all the other piers, privately owned or municipal, are white.

That first summer on the north shore, Alexa and I were introduced to a new summer activity and ritual. We were each handed a paint brush and several gallons of white paint and pointed toward our pier. From that June before eighth grade until the September when I left for college, the first order of business every summer was painting the pier. I don't even want to think about the gallons of white paint we went through, or the limitless paint brushes, rollers, stir sticks, and cans of turpentine.

Alexa and I toiled out on the pier under the sun from early morning until it was time to clean up for dinner. I think it took us weeks to get the pier painted that first year.

We fought over who got to use the roller for the planks (easy part) and who had to use the brush to paint the posts (annoyingly hard part). Eventually, we worked out a system of daily trade-offs between the roller and the brush. We also kept meticulous track of how many posts we had each painted. Foul was called on anyone who spent a whole afternoon painting a single post. Occasionally, things got ugly.

By the time the job was finally complete, our legs, arms, and faces were a bizarrely-mottled mosaic of tan and pale, created by paint splatters that we never quite had the patience to rub off with turpentine.

A technological break-through occurred in our pier painting when I was fifteen. By that time, Alexa and I had the annual job down to a science. Post-versus-plank duties were agreed to on Day One, and we adhered to a strict start-to-finish timeline of three days maximum. We piled all our supplies into the wagon of the family Wheel Horse lawn tractor, stripped down to our bikinis, fired up the transistor radio, and careened with our booty across the lawn and down to the pier.

If we had to paint the pier, at least we would use it as the first chance to get our tans going.

The critical scientific advancement in our lives was latex paint. We no longer had to worry about keeping the paint on the pier and off of us. This added an important, new aspect to pier painting—the paint fight.

It inevitably started with one of us accidentally stepping or sitting in the other's just-finished paint job. It always ended in rollers full of paint being rolled up legs, and thick, dripping brushes smacked across arms and stomachs. When we'd made a complete mess of each other and the pier, we jumped in the lake to rise it all off.

Today the idea of rising paint off in the lake is unthinkable. But it was the late 60s and early 70s. Joni Mitchell hadn't written

Big Yellow Taxi yet, and we all believed that the springs that shoot cold, fresh water up from the lake's bottom kept it rejuvenated.

Rinsing latex paint of wasn't the only ecologically unfriendly thing I did in those years. I admit that I washed my hair in the lake all summer long, believing that the lake water left it softer and shinier.

Our pier painting had to be completed before June fifteenth, when Mail Boat deliveries started. As always, we set our schedule by its prompt arrival. Because we now lived closer to town and on the north shore, the Mail Boat arrived at our pier earlier in the day, and we adjusted quickly to this new schedule.

The summer before, in 1967, Gage Marine had retired the *Walworth* and introduced a new Mail Boat, the *Walworth II.* Compared to the charm of the original *Walworth,* the *Walworth II* seemed a bit like Shrek to me. Rather than sleek wood, it had a steel hull and sported a motif of powder blue and white. It rode far higher in the water, and the higher sides closed in the passengers more than the old *Walworth.* It also had a second deck above the main deck that nearly doubled the passenger capacity.

The new *Walworth II* was built by Schwartz Marine. It weighed sixty tons and was sixty feet long with a fourteen-foot beam. Rather than a single engine and propeller, this new Mail Boat sported twin-diesel, 5208-horsepower engines, making it much more powerful, and importantly, more agile than its predecessor. It was designed with elements uniquely crafted to assist with the mail delivery. Next to the captain's chair, they installed a cabinet specifically designed to hold mail deliveries. In addition, Gage had asked Schwartz to design a unique rub rail on the starboard side of the boat. It was higher on the boat's side than a rub rail would normally be, and was about fifteen inches wide, giving the Mail Jumper a more generous landing pad.

The *Walworth II* may not have been as elegant as its namesake, but it was highly functional. It could go out in rougher waters, and provided better shelter to passengers via the higher sides and drop down plastic windows for rainy or windy days. The mail needed to be delivered no matter what the weather, and the *Walworth II* was built to endure more, and be safer, during those deliveries.

That first summer, as I made my transition from Summer Girl to Local Girl, I existed very much in a state of limbo between those two worlds. As I have said, you can't be both a local and a summer person in Lake Geneva, but that summer I floated someplace between the two—not living quite as I had in past summers, but not yet a part of the local community. One constant was the Mail Boat's daily passing. But when Labor Day arrived, instead of packing up and heading back to the city, I prepared to become a real, fulltime, resident of Lake Geneva.

WOODS SCHOOL AND RIOTS

It was time to go back to school.

Along with Alexa and my brother, Andrew, I would be attending Woods School. Woods is located on the north side of the lake at the intersection of Highway 50 and the western most entrance to Snake Road. The school opened in 1868 for the children of Irish immigrants who were arriving in the area. Containing the full complement of grades from pre-kindergarten through eighth grade, today Woods School serves one hundred and forty-nine students. When I entered the eighth grade in the fall of 1968, the student body was less than sixty.

In River Forest, my seventh grade class had one hundred and twenty other students. At Woods, my eighth grade class totaled seven. We shared a room, and teacher, with the other twelve students who made up the sixth and seventh grades. Andrew was entering kindergarten. Alexa was in the sixth grade and shared my classroom.

There was definitely some culture shock.

We were not the only new students at Woods School. The Draper family had also moved to the lake on a year-round basis. They lived about a mile west of us on the lake. Their house, Glen Fern, was a beautiful, Beaux Arts granite mansion built in 1911 by N.C. Sears, an Illinois Appellate Court judge and member of Northwestern University's Law faculty.

Although a mile away, the Drapers were our closest year-round neighbors. Dan was in eighth grade with me, and his sister, Drew, was in Alexa's sixth grade class. Their two younger sisters were also Wood School attendees. Jointly, our families' total of seven children accounted for fifteen percent of the student body at Woods School. We quickly became fast friends.

Decades later, five of the Draper/Kanelos clan reunited for dinner one night in Boca Raton, Florida. Recounting our Woods School days, we sent a photo into the *Lake Geneva Regional News* with a note that a Woods School reunion had taken place. The picture was promptly published, which has always been one of the wonderful things about a small town. Just about everything counts as important in some way.

Though small, Woods had a beautiful, recently built gymnasium funded by a donation from Lee Phillip Bell. Lee Phillip was the star of the Lee Phillip Show in Chicago, and her husband William J. Bell was a television producer. Together, the Bells created the well-known soap opera *The Young and The Restless (Y&R)*. In addition to their Spanish-style lakefront estate, Casa del Suena, they owned Sunset Farm adjacent to Woods School. *Y&R*, which received a Daytime Emmy Award in 1975, takes place in the fictional town of Genoa City, named after Lake Geneva's closest neighboring town.

The year 1968 became 1969, and the world was ablaze with change. Every paper I wrote in eighth grade at Woods School was in some way related to the change that was happening all around us. It was impossible not to be affected by it—the first man landing on the moon, Woodstock, Vietnam War protests, the draft lottery, Charles Manson, Women's Liberation, Chappaquiddick, the Chicago Seven, and Black Power. And that was only part of the list.

Two summers before, in 1967, summer fun in the town of Lake Geneva had erupted into riots. Nine thousand partying, college-age youths—nearly twice the population of Lake Geneva—turned angry and violent, tearing down a statue in one of the lakeside parks, throwing bottles and cans, breaking windows, and damaging public and private property. The National Guard was mobilized. It was a sign of the cultural changes that America was going through, and I was banned from going into town for the rest of the summer.

Despite all these distractions, I managed to graduate as the "valedictorian" of our seven person class. Then it was summer again.

That summer, like the one before it, was spent primarily at home and on the lake. Alexa and I often walked along the lake path to the Draper house. But the Whaler provided unlimited access to whatever I could find to do on the water or its shores. It was like a door was thrown wide open, and I ran through it with gusto, finding endless things to do. I continued my place in limbo between being a Summer Girl and a local. Everyone I knew—other than my handful of Woods School friends—were still summer people. Everyone I had access to—either via the Whaler or the lake path, except for the Drapers—were summer residents. So, although we now lived at the lake year round, we still lived within the world of our summer connections.

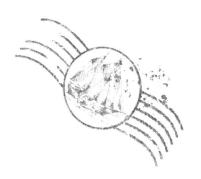

Local Girl

When I started high school in the fall of 1969, I completed my transition to Local Girl. Badger High School sits just southeast of the town of Lake Geneva and serves the communities of Lake Geneva and Genoa City. With two hundred and thirty-two students in my class, it introduced me, really for the first time, to the locals. I made new friends, joined clubs, went to football games and slowly, but surely, became a local.

As always when summer arrived, the first order of business was to paint the pier. Then there were tennis lessons, and an enduring crush on my tennis teacher, Larry, which ran from year to year. A significant amount of time was spent hanging out on the pier with my portable radio, a variety of paperbacks, and a lifetime supply of baby oil.

One summer, I rigged one of our floating lawn chairs with a line of yellow marine rope and a five pound anchor. After setting my transistor radio to the best station and adjusting it for ideal reception on the pier, I settled myself into the lawn chair with my massive paperback version of *Gone with the Wind*, paddled myself about twenty feet from the pier and shore, and dropped anchor. I stayed there most of the day, and the next, and for about another two weeks, while I finished *Gone with the Wind*. It was the best fly swatter I ever read.

I no longer waited with baited breath for the Mail Jumper. I had learned to be more subtle than that. I still knew what time the Mail Boat delivered to our pier and I still made a point of picking up the mail every day. I liked to time things so that I would be trotting down the pier stairs just as the Mail Boat slid by. That way, I could give the tourists a friendly wave without paying too much attention to the Mail Boy.

The summer nights were often hot and muggy, and our house wasn't air-conditioned. My parents installed window air conditioners in their bedroom and in Andrew's room, which faced the back of the house. But Alexa, Jorjanne, and I, with lake-facing rooms, were out of luck. The lake breeze was supposed to be our air conditioning.

Although my bed was within inches of the window, there were nights when the air was deadly still, the humidity was sky high, and the house was stifling. On those nights, trying to sleep was unbearable. Usually, Alexa gave up before I did, and went to sleep on the sofa in the screened, summer porch. By the time I finally gave up and abandoned our bedroom, there was really no place left in the house to get relief. Unable to sleep, I often walked down to the lake and sat on the end of the pier with my feet dangling in the water while I listened to conversations across the Narrows. Sometimes I striped off my PJs and took a swim. On other hot nights, I dug the jib sheet out of the sail boat and, wrapping up in it, would fall asleep in the back of the Gage-Hacker while it hung from the hoist in the boat slip.

MANURE CITY AND FOUR HUNDRED TENNIS BALLS

Besides painting the pier, Alexa and I were tasked with another annual summer chore—mucking out the stables.

As was the tradition around the lake, when my family bought Tanglewood we also inherited Ted Casper, Nathan Hunt's caretaker. Ted, his wife, and son no longer lived in the apartment Hunt had added to the house in the fifties. That part of the house was now our breakfast room, family room, Jorjanne's bedroom, and the bathroom that Alexa, Jorjanne, and I shared. But Ted was still working for Hunt when we bought the house and, therefore, became our gardener and caretaker.

Along with other duties around the property, Ted took care of the horses. But every summer, without fail, my father would announce that the stalls needed to be mucked out down to their clay base. Somehow, like painting the pier, this task was never assigned to anyone but Alexa and me.

For two or three days from dawn to dusk, we would shovel straw and horse poop out of the stalls and into the wagon of our trusty Wheel Horse lawn tractor. We filled dozens of loads and then drove them, one by one, to an area in the woods that we christened "Manure City" as the piles of spent straw grew and grew.

After hours of back breaking work, combined with inhaling high levels of ammonia, we became completely slap-happy. By three in the afternoon on "mucking" days, we would be hysterical over idiotic jokes and near misses with pitchforks. Then, of course, when we were done for the day, we jumped in the lake to cool down, and rinse off the sweat and dirt.

One summer evening my dad, infuriated because he had come home planning to play tennis—only to find that there were no tennis balls—sent us out to find the four hundred tennis balls he was sure he had purchased at the start of the summer. After an hour or so of combing the woods that surrounded the tennis courts on three sides, we had found twelve. Banned from re-entering the house without several hundred neon-green tennis balls, we sat on the edge of the court making up stories about the possible fates of the missing three hundred and eighty-eight balls, and laughing late into the night.

During those summers, laughter was the coin in which we traded. Whatever happened, no matter how exhausting, aggravating, or seemingly unfair to our teenage minds, Alexa and I could only laugh in the end.

SAILING SCHOOL AND LEMONADE

My sixteenth summer, my dad bought an M-20 sailboat. We had always sailed the family Sunfish, a small, easy-to-handle, single-sail boat with a clip-on rudder and center board. But this was a sail boat of a different color.

The M-20 scow is a flat bottomed sailboat that was designed in Lake Geneva by Harry Melges Sr. and Harry (Buddy) Melges Jr. Buddy is internationally known for representing the Chicago Yacht Club in the 1987 America's Cup race as the captain of *Heart of America*. Racing again in 1992, Buddy won the America's Cup on *America 3*.

An M-20 is twenty feet long and requires a crew of two. It has a single mast that supports a mainsail, jib, and, as needed, a spinnaker. Thanks in part to the Melges family, and other great local sailors, Lake Geneva is renowned as one of the country's top scow sailing centers. On most Sundays during the summer, you can see races being held in the open waters between the Lake Geneva Yacht Club, Conference Point, and Cedar Point.

Our M-20 seemed to just appear on a Shore Station beside the pier one day. The next night at dinner, my dad announced that Alexa and I should learn to sail it. Certainly, he declared, there were classes at the Yacht Club for which we could sign up.

Well, there were. And sign up we did. For the only class that let you bring your own boat: the M-20 Racing Class. On the Tuesday before the 4th of July, Alexa and I tied the M-20 behind the Whaler, and hauled it across and down the lake to the club.

We were feeling quite pleased with ourselves about how well we did getting our new sailboat there successfully, when we walked into the class to find that our Woods School friends, Dan and Drew Draper, had also signed up for the class.

All happy coincidences ended there.

As it turned out, the racing class we had signed up for was targeted to highly-experienced, teen-age sailors who wanted to refine their racing expertise—not beginners who happened to have their own boat. Dan and Drew knew how to sail an M-20. They knew how to hoist a spinnaker, and what the terms "jibe" and "come about" meant.

Alexa and I didn't have a clue.

So when, twenty minutes into that first class, our instructor announced that everyone was to go out to their boat and rig up, we were definitely in trouble.

But would we admit our shortcomings?

Absolutely not.

We gamely went out to the water, got in the boat, and tried to sneak peeks at what everyone else was doing, and in which order. The jig was up when we couldn't even figure out how to raise the mainsail. This, by the way, is not rocket science, but it was a lot more complex than pulling up the sail on our little Sunfish.

With some help, we got the sails hoisted and the boat out

into open water. (All the while, I might add, providing Total Entertainment to the growing group of spectators on the shore.) If there had been any question about what level of sailor we were when we walked in that morning, there wasn't by the end of the day.

But Alexa and I stayed in the class. Twice a week for eight weeks, we made complete fools of ourselves at the Lake Geneva Yacht Club. We tipped our boat over so many times they claimed it was a club record. We turtled the boat three times (tipped it over on its side and then completely upside down—a supposedly rare occurrence with scows), and had to be rescued by the Water Safety Patrol twice. Once, I knocked Alexa completely out of the boat because I couldn't decide which direction to turn the boat and yelled out the wrong instructions, so she had no idea she needed to duck when the fifteen-foot boom whiplashed across the boat and knocked her silly.

It was harder than hell to turn the boat around by myself and sail back to her. And, believe me, the conversation as I pulled her back into the boat wasn't one any of you would want to have heard.

Sailing school was a debacle of enormous proportions for us. But we kept at it. We decided that racing wasn't in our future, and adopted a "Make the Best of It" attitude.

We began to bring lemonade, sandwiches, and a radio along with us on the boat. We relaxed and soaked in the sunshine. It was a given that we would come in last. The challenge was whether we would finish the race at all. But we were alive and upright for the moment, and that was reason for continuous celebration.

The very last race of the season, in what I can only term a complete aberration, somehow Alexa and I were headed to the finish line not in last place, but about to come in second to last.

This was a complete surprise not just to us, but to our instructor, the race official, and the rest of the class. At the helm, I was sailing just a tip ahead of one of our classmate boats when someone in the judge's boat started chanting encouragement through the bullhorn. I blame that distraction for making me lose my concentration just long enough for the other boat to slip ahead of us, leaving us, once again, to come in last.

But Alexa and I didn't care—we had survived the race, the class, and the summer!

EDGEWOOD AND ADVENTURES

One day that same summer, a boat pulled up to our pier loaded with three women who were making an impromptu visit to see my mom. This was not something that happened regularly. In fact, I'm certain that it was the only time in my life that a boat full of women appeared at our pier looking for my mother, which is probably why it has stuck so clearly in my mind all these years.

At some point during the visit, one of the women mentioned that she and her husband were moving their family to the lake fulltime, and that one of her daughters would be entering as a junior at Badger High with me.

I spotted her daughter on the first day of school a few weeks later, sitting at a meeting in the Badger gymnasium. Nancy Geldermann, along with her four brothers, three sisters, mom, dad, two dogs, cat—and a bit later—six guinea fowl, four peacocks, and two swans, had arrived as a new Local Girl.

We immediately became best friends.

Nancy and her family lived slightly farther away from me than the Drapers and in the opposite direction, but I could make the shore walk between our houses in about twenty-five minutes.

Like mine, her house was on Snake Road, but it was down one of the more elegantly landscaped drives. Also like mine, her house and its property had a name, Edgewood.

Edgewood was built in 1907 by Edward F. Swift, one of eleven children of Gustavus F. Swift, founder of Swift and Company meatpacking. Like so many of the elite families with estates on the lake, Edward Swift's family and company were based in Chicago. For Swift and Co., the Chicago Union Stockyards provided the raw materials used to create many of Swift's products including Lazy Maple bacon and Brown'N Serve breakfast sausage. Many years later, Swift and Co. would create the Butterball turkey.

Edgewood was designed by Howard Van Doren Shaw, the same architect who designed Alta Vista, the estate just two doors down the lake from my house. Originally named Villa Hortensia after Edward's wife, the Swift family summered there for fifteen years. Then, over the next fifty years, the home passed through the hands of three other owners, and was renamed several times.

Just prior to the Geldermann family's arrival, the estate was the summer home of George F. Getz, Jr., owner and President of the Globe Corporation. Getz transitioned his father's successful coal business into a manufacturing success. Later the Globe Corporation transitioned again, this time into an investment and real estate stronghold that is still owned and run by the Getz family. George was on the Board of Directors of the Chicago Cubs and instrumental in starting the Water Safety Patrol, which over ninety years later, remains the primary resource for ensuring the safety of swimmers and boaters on Lake Geneva.

In 1972, Nancy's father, Thomas A. Geldermann, a Chicago Board of Trade commodities trader, bought the estate from George Getz, and the family became year-round residents.

Despite living on a significant Lake Geneva estate, Nancy

drove a red, Plymouth Valiant that required a plug-in engine-block heater to start in the winter, and a lot of positive thinking to entice the engine to turn over in the summer, spring, and fall.

But a plug-in car was better than no car, which is what I had.

Early in our senior year, the Valiant finally gave out and she inherited her brother's two-door, manual, Opal GT. A manual transmission was new to Nancy, but I assured her I knew how to drive a stick shift. This confidence was based on a maximum of three lessons in our household Ford pickup truck which, clearly, was not the same experience. While she handled steering, clutch, and gas, I manned the gear shift. Thus we both learned to drive a stick shift while driving up and down Snake Road.

We had many similarly suspect adventures. One of the most memorable was our trip to another Lake Geneva landmark, Wadsworth Hall.

Wadsworth Hall is the estate directly to the west of Edgewood. We passed its imposing entrance on Snake Road several times a day during the school year. In the summers, if I walked over to Nancy's on the lake path, I always crossed Wadsworth Hall's vast lawn. The estate was immaculate, and stunningly beautiful, but always quiet.

Like my house, it was designed in the Georgian style, but on a far, far grander scale. Built for Norman W. Harris of Chicago's Harris Trust and Savings Bank in 1906, it has long been considered the most beautiful estate on the lake. The grounds were designed by the Olmstead Brothers, sons of Frederick Law Olmstead, who created New York City's Central Park, the Capitol Grounds in Washington D.C., and the grounds for the 1893 Columbian Exposition in Chicago.

In 1920, the estate was purchased by Walden W. Shaw, founder of the Yellow Taxi Cab Company in Chicago, and renamed The

Stennings. By the 1930s, it had passed to Shaw's son-in-law, Daniel F. Peterkin, Jr., who had married his daughter, Bessie, in 1929. Peterkin eventually became President and Chairman of the Morton Salt Company.

In 1973, our senior year of high school, The Stennings, which everyone continued to call Wadsworth Hall, was still owned by Daniel Peterkin. Mr. Peterkin was sixty-seven, and had recently retired from the leadership of Morton Salt.

He was a man of mystery to Nancy and me. Her parents had occasional conversations with Mr. Peterkin, as they did with the Wrigley families who owned several lakefront properties adjacent to Edgewood on the east. But it was Wadsworth Hall and Daniel Peterkin that engaged our imaginations.

What did Wadsworth Hall look like inside? What was *he* like?

Taken as individuals, Nancy and I were each fully capable of coming up with any number of somewhat hare-brained ideas, but as a rule, others were able to dissuade us from executing those ideas. When Nancy and I were together, however, we thought each other's ideas were fabulous! This led to a significant number of half-baked plans being carried out.

Our trip to Wadsworth Hall was one.

It was a late autumn afternoon and we were hanging around Edgewood's kitchen where her mother and siblings generally gathered. Somehow the Peterkin name came up, and when the group dispersed to other activities, Nancy and I hit upon our brilliant idea—we would pay a visit to Wadsworth Hall. Right now. What better time to make a casual, and neighborly, little visit to say hello as the new neighbors?

Never mind that I was not a new neighbor. In fact, I was really not a neighbor at all, but the Geldermanns had only lived there for a year—which sounded passably new—and Nancy was one of them. In order to make things look more legitimate, we whipped up a batch of brownies and threw them in the oven. We really couldn't wait the thirty-five minute cooking time required by the recipe to execute our plan, so we pulled the brownies out—quite literally as half-baked as our plan.

Runny brownies in hand, we threw on our parkas and plunged through the woods that separated the two estates. It took us a while to find the front door (which was naturally on the back of the house). It was already dark when we rang the bell.

We didn't ring once or twice. No, we kept on ringing and ringing for a good eight or nine minutes, just in case. Really, despite the fact that it seemed like no one was ever at Wadsworth Hall, at that moment we just couldn't believe that no one would be home.

We were just about to finally give up when there was a noise or two, and then the door creaked open. (Well, it seemed like it creaked to us.) We were greeted by someone who was clearly part of Mr. Peterkin's staff. We cheerfully gave her our message: "We are your new next door neighbors, and we've come by to say hello. And—look! We've brought brownies!!" (Which were mashed into tin foil that was now bent in about five different directions due to our trek through the woods.)

She asked us to wait and left us at the door for another five minutes. Then she returned, took the brownies in hand, and ushered us into the massive living room.

Thus began the evening we spent with Daniel Peterkin.

We stayed for about two hours, and the encounter remains one of those special moments when you know you are being given a glimpse of something special and rare.

At first, we sat in the living room chatting about how the Geldermanns were settling in. Then he started telling us tales.

Fabulous stories of his life that included a monkey he'd kept as a pet, and which used to run through the elegant mansion causing trouble; and the seaplanes he had owned, landed on the lake, and then parked at his pier.

He was in the middle of compiling all the photos from various travels and adventures, so we paged through many of his albums, and examined the large boards he'd put up to help organize the photography. We went upstairs to see some of the rooms, and then back down to the living room. When we finally left, we were ecstatic with the success of our adventure.

I'm sure her parents were mortified by our chutzpa. But for Nancy and me, the evening was memorable. Daniel Peterkin had been a warm and engaging host, despite the fact that I'm sure he was fairly entertained, and not at all fooled, by the two of us. We never saw the brownies. And once we were back at Edgewood, we agreed that Mr. Peterkin's assistant looked smart enough to have dumped them directly into the trash.

Wadsworth Hall stayed in the Peterkin family for nearly eighty years. It was sold in 1999 to investment manager Richard Driehaus, who renamed the estate Glenworth Gardens.

Books and Freedom

I have always been a voracious reader. In grade school, I was obsessed with stories about horses and historical biographies. I checked out *Misty of Chincoteague* and the biographies of Dolly Madison and Abraham Lincoln more than nine times each and could recite passages from all the *Black Stallion* books.

In high school, my reading headed in new directions. One of the books I picked up was *The Feminine Mystique* by Betty Friedan. Women's rights had been a major political issue since my middle school years. The Equal Rights Amendment had struggled to win passage for years before it finally was passed in 1972, and I often used it as my subject for history and political science papers.

Women's rights seemed obvious to me. I painted piers, and hauled manure. I was the editor of the school newspaper. My athletic endeavors weren't separated into boy's teams and girl's teams, they were out on the lake and in the fields—water skiing, sailing, swimming, and horseback riding. I was blissfully oblivious to boundaries established by stereotypes. I had always been expected to do whatever was needed, and I expected myself to be physically able to do anything I wanted to do. At seventeen, I knew what a socket wrench was, and how to use the electric drill. I could drive the lawn tractor, pump gas for the boat, and clean the paint brushes. At the same time, I read *Seventeen Magazine*, had a wonderful boyfriend, and loved to dance every Friday night at the YMCA. But Women's Liberation, and bringing change to old traditions, would soon play an important role in my life.

I graduated from Badger in 1973, and that summer, while not my last in Lake Geneva by a long shot, was the last summer that my Badger High School group was all together. We were celebrating graduation, and enjoying being the big shots we thought we were.

Most of my fellow classmates had summer jobs. Nancy was life guarding for the Water Safety Patrol along with several of my other friends. Dick Payne was working for Elmer Zingle, renting boats at the Riviera pier. Others were working at the sporting goods store, Arnold's Pharmacy, or caddying at local country clubs. I was one of the few who didn't have a summer job. My dad was happy to have Alexa and I handle the painting and mucking jobs at home, and once those were completed, I was free for the summer.

I was on the lake that summer more than ever. I was driving the Gage-Hacker now, which meant that I could pull water skiers and the gigantic, tractor-tire inner tubes we bought, inflated, and piled two or three people onto for crazy rides behind the boat. Some mornings I was up by five-thirty, picking up friends to enjoy an hour of water skiing while the lake was still glassy and quiet. Most days, I would take the boat to Fontana, pick up Nancy, and eat lunch with her at the Yacht Club or Abbey Springs. Then I'd cruise to the opposite end of the lake, and pick up whoever had a day off for an afternoon of water skiing and tubing. Just before dinner, the water would go glassy again, and I would get in one more turn on the water ski before heading home.

My boyfriend, Mark, and his family had moved to the lake year-round the previous fall. The O'Donoghues broke our local isolation barrier in a big way. They moved into the house two doors west of us a few weeks before I started my senior year at Badger. There were seven O'Donoghue kids, the oldest—Tom and Bill—were in college. The youngest Tim and Maureen were in the single digits.

The first day of school, Alexa and I had our first chance to meet Mark, and his sister, Jean, who now shared our bus stop on Chapin Road. Within a few weeks, Mark and I became boyfriend and girlfriend. James, Tim, and Maureen O'Donoghue were enrolled at Woods School, where James and my brother would become lifelong friends.

There were plenty of O'Donoghue antics that year, including bowling balls dropped out of second story bedroom windows. Like us, the O'Donoghues had horses, and related chores were split within the family. The summer after my graduation, Mark and his brother, Bill who was home for the summer from Marquette University, were retained for summer duties at their house the same way that Alexa and I were at ours.

In July, there was the debacle of the O'Donoghue hornet nest.

A mud dabber nest had been discovered in the attic of the O'Donoghue house early in the summer, and for several weeks Mark and Bill noodled on the best strategy for getting rid of the hornets so that the nest could be removed. The idea that they finally came up with, and executed, was straight out of *Ghostbusters Goes Wild* (yet to be made).

Here was their plan.

Buy large quantities of bug spray. Get everyone else to leave the house for the afternoon. Protect themselves from potentially angry hornets by dressing in one-piece snowmobile suits, helmets, gloves, and boots.

They decided to execute their plan at high noon.

It was July. It was ninety degrees.

What I saw from out on the lake as I approached the O'Donoghue pier in my boat that day was two, six-foot crazies, swathed from head-to-toe in black snowmobile outfits and helmets, fleeing across their ranch-house roof as fast as their snowmobile boots would take them.

They were crazy. I loved that.

The summer, as it always did, flew by, and in late August I left—just as I had when I was a Summer Girl. Except, this time, I was headed for Boulder, and the freshman class at the University of Colorado.

Westgate was built in 1917 by Gertrude Allen who died before construction was complete. This lakeside view is from the 1950s.

The back yard at Westgate, 1959. I am headed to the lake in my scarf, while my sister, Alexa, assesses the situation from the driveway.

My parents, Alice and George Kanelos, pose with my sister,
Jorjanne, and me, on the Westgate pier in 1956.

On the Westgate pier again, three years later, in 1959. I am in
the striped life vest with my mother, Alexa, and Jorjanne.

A view from the lake of our house at 668 South Lake Shore
Drive. We spent long hours wading in from the sand beach
to hunt for crawfish, skipping stones, and snails.

Our pier at 668 South Lake Shore Drive, the narrow section on the left is
where the mailbox was located. The pier width, and the angle at which
the *Walworth* had to approach, made it one of the harder piers to jump.

Launched in 1916, the original *Walworth* served as the US Mail Boat for over sixty years. Here the Mail Jumper prepares for his next delivery. (Photo courtesy of Lake Geneva Cruise Line.)

Built in 1967, the *Walworth II* was designed specifically to deliver the mail on Lake Geneva. (Photo courtesy of Lake Geneva Cruise Line.)

Tanglewood is two doors west of Alta Vista, on the north shore of the lake, very close to the Narrows. My family moved here in 1968, when I was twelve years old.

A view of Tanglewood from the backyard looking toward the three car garage and front door. The low, brick wall, and the rose garden behind, it created a wonderful entryway to the house.

Sitting on the pier at Tanglewood with Mark O'Donoghue
in 1973, just after my graduation from Badger High School.
To our right, you can see our marine delivery mailbox.
Behind us, the Gage-Hacker sits up on its hoist.

Edgewood, circa 1975, when it was the home of the Thomas
Geldermann family, and my best friend, Nancy Geldermann
Williams. I was at Edgewood so much that her siblings started
calling me 'sis.' (Photo courtesy of Nancy Geldermann Williams.)

Glen Fern, built in 1911, was the home of my Woods School friends Dan and Drew Draper. Glen Fern was less than a mile walk from our house along the lake path. (Photo courtesy of Lake Geneva Public Library.)

The Riviera municipal building and docks, where I spent all four summers during college—first working as the Mail Girl, and then as the dispatcher for the Water Safety Patrol. (Doug Ward Photography, LLC.)

Waterskiing, my favorite summertime activity, in 1976. My treasured mahogany O'Brien slalom ski was a gift from my YiaYia (grandmother). Waterskiing without a life vest is both illegal and unsafe, and I should have known better. I have no excuse.

This publicity photo, taken the first day I ever jumped, shows me putting mail into my own mailbox. It and has been featured in newspapers, magazines, the internet, and on television around the world. (Photo courtesy of Lake Geneva Cruise Line.)

Another publicity shot taken the first day I ever tried mail jumping. I'm standing on the rub rail that runs along the outside of the *Walworth II*. Lake Geneva Cruise Line built several special features into the boat specifically for marine mail delivery. The young boy watching from inside is Bill Gage, Jr. Today, Bill is the third-generation owner of both Gage Marine and the Lake Geneva Cruise Line.

Elaine Kanelas demonstrates her techniques as the new "mailboy" for houses around Lake Geneva, Wis. She gets ready (above), leaps from the sight-seeing boat (left), delivers the mail and leaps aboard the moving boat (far left).

It's mail by aquabatics

One of the many newspaper articles that appeared about Lake Geneva's marine mail delivery, and the first Mail Girl. This ran in the June 6-7, 1974, issue of the *Chicago Daily News* during my first year jumping. The head peering out of the *Walworth II* is Bill Gage, Sr., who believed in me, and my desire to be the first Mail Girl, enough to give me the job of my dreams.

A great view of Mail Jumper, Bob Kirkland, circa early 1970s. From this angle you can see just how much air and water has to be traversed to get back on the boat. (Photo courtesy of Lake Geneva Cruise Line.)

Elyse Geldermann, circa late 1970s. The large quantity of mail delivered at the summer camps along the lakeshore requires a canvas bag and a handoff to get delivered. (Photo courtesy of Lake Geneva Cruise Line.)

Ceylon Court was transported, re-assembled, and then expanded on the lake by Frank R. Chandler and his wife. Originally part of the Ceylonese exhibit at the 1893 Chicago World Fair, the house was razed in 1958, and replaced by Ceylon Point. (Photo courtesy of Lake Geneva Public Library.)

My family moved to Ceylon Point late in 1976. When I lived there, the entire point was our front lawn providing incredible views down the entire length of the lake. Late afternoons were stunning from the house's vantage point.

The back of Ceylon Point and its front door. My bedroom, with its beautiful bay window, was just above the entry overlooking the fountain.

The lifeguards, swimming instructors, and boat crew of the Water Safety Patrol pose for the annual photo early in the morning in 1977. I am front row center. This picture is populated with so many of my friends that it would take too long to list everyone. Behind us, the *Belle of the Lake* and *Lady of the Lake* wait for the day's passengers.

Lake Geneva Cruise Line renovated the *Walworth II* from
top to bottom in 2004. It underwent another major update
in 2014. (Photo courtesy of Lake Geneva Cruise Line.)

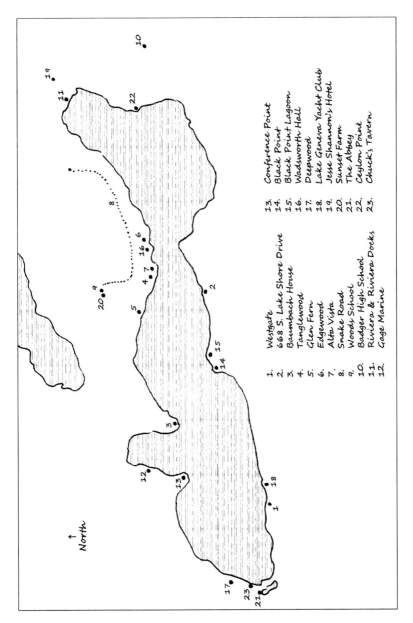

1. Westgate
2. 668 S. Lake Shore Drive
3. Baumbach House
4. Tanglewood
5. Glen Fern
6. Edgewood
7. Alta Vista
8. Snake Road
9. Woods School
10. Badger High School
11. Riviera & Riviera Docks
12. Gage Marine
13. Conference Point
14. Black Point
15. Black Point Lagoon
16. Wadsworth Hall
17. Deepwood
18. Lake Geneva Yacht Club
19. Jesse Shannon's Hotel
20. Sunset Farm
21. The Abbey
22. Ceylon Point
23. Chuck's Tavern

North

Credit: Image created by Kelly Morrison

Mail Girl

C ollege was wonderful. Boulder had much milder winters than Wisconsin, a good football team (at that time), and twenty-four thousand students. Most of my Badger classmates were attending University of Wisconsin schools, with a few headed to Northwestern, or the University of Chicago. Nancy went to Arizona, and Mark O'Donoghue started his senior year at Badger High.

I moved into Nichols Hall on the Boulder campus, joined Delta Gamma sorority, ice skated almost daily at the CU Rec Center, and took classes with the intention of becoming a journalist. Before I knew it, spring had arrived, and I started thinking about the summer. And I knew exactly the job I wanted for the summer—I wanted to jump the mail!

The problem was that only boys jumped the mail. But I had wanted that job—that experience, really—since I was a six-year-old and there was no way that I was letting something as minor as a sixty-eight year old tradition stand in my way.

I used Women's Liberation and very significant, social change it was creating as a springboard for my application. I wrote a letter to Bill Gage, suggesting that it was time for a girl to jump the mail, and stated that I wanted to be that girl. It was a bold and somewhat crazy thing for me to do, but bold-and-crazy might as well be my middle name.

The Gages and everyone involved in the US Mail Boat could have taken my idea as just that—a crazy idea. But they didn't. And about three weeks later, I received a letter from Bill saying that I was hired.

To say that I was ecstatic would be an enormous understatement.

First Jumps and Photographers

I arrived home at the end of May and immediately checked in with Bill Gage. As the Mail Girl, I would be working at Gage Marine's Riviera dock location, which was completely different from the Gage Marine Williams Bay boatyard I knew so well. The Riviera operation consisted of a small office for the manager, the ticket office, and the excursion boats.

Bill told me to meet him at the Riviera dock the following week dressed for work. "Dressed for work" meant one thing to me: shopping. I needed Mail Girl clothes. Gage wanted me in red, white, and blue jump-appropriate outfits. I bought white and navy shorts, tennis skirts, and culottes; all paired with similarly-themed tops. I had ensembles for warm, hot, chilly, and rainy weather. But the most important item in my Mail Girl wardrobe was my shoes.

I'd grown up jumping on and off boats—not big excursion-sized boats—but boats none-the-less. Regardless of the size of your boat, when you tie-up at, or pull away from, a pier, there is always an element of jumping from the boat to the pier involved. Because of that, I knew exactly what shoes I needed: Sperry Top-siders.

If you live on or near Lake Geneva, you own Top-siders. So do sailors and boaters around the world.

Top-siders are legendary for their ability to maintain grip on slick docks and boats. Created in 1935 by Paul Sperry, the rubber sole of Top-siders are tooled with a pattern of tightly-spaced, wave-like grooves that work like the bottom of a dog's paw to create grip. I got my first pair in the middle of high school, and now three years later, they were just about worn in enough to be perfect. Top-siders tend to be somewhat indestructible and within my group of friends, it was important that your Top-siders look like they had lived a full and useful life. Sometimes this meant taking drastic measures to give them a well-worn look.

My apparel and foot-wear ready, I dutifully arrived at the Gage office on the Riviera dock. The Riviera was built in 1932 as part of the Federal Work Projects Administration (WPA), the most extensive and ambitious of Franklin D. Roosevelt's New Deal agencies. The mission of the WPA was to construct public buildings and roadways as a way of providing employment during the Great Depression. WPA buildings were built in nearly every municipality across the United States.

In Lake Geneva, the WPA funded construction of the Lake Geneva Municipal Building, later known as the Riviera. The Riv is on the US Register of Historic Places. It sits on a man-made peninsula created with two hundred and eighty wood pilings sunk into bedrock beneath the lake. It was built, along with the Lake Geneva Municipal Beach, to provide the town of Lake Geneva's citizenry with access to the lakefront. Completed at the height of the Swing Era, the building included a ballroom that hosted bands led by Louie Armstrong, Artie Shaw, and the Dorsey brothers.

My first day on the job as the Mail Girl was a gorgeous, early June day, the kind of day that everyone waits all winter to experience. I was only a few, short weeks away from the June fifteenth start of mail delivery, and there was a lot for me to learn.

The first order of business was my introduction to Harold Friestad. Harold was the first official boss I would ever have, and as of 2014, he is still running the Lake Geneva Cruise Line. No one could ask for a nicer, or more dedicated, boss. Harold is an icon of Lake Geneva, who started his career with Gage in 1960, while he was a student at Milton College in Milton, Wisconsin. He drove the original *Walworth* on mail runs. Undoubtedly, he was at the helm many times while my childhood-self watched the mail being delivered.

His only break in service at Gage was for two years after he graduated from college in 1963. By 1968, he had returned to Gage and was the General Manager of Lake Geneva Cruise Line. Today, Harold is Vice President and General Manager of the company. He's responsible for scheduling, and staffing, six tour boats, as well as private charters, and a landside tour service. His annual summertime staff totals more than one hundred, but only about fifty percent are students. The remainder are teachers and other locals who work seasonally at Gage, often for decades. Harold has four year-round staff members as well, who handle long-range planning for the high season. He has been honored as Citizen of the Year by both the Lake Geneva Convention and Visitors Bureau and the Fontana Chamber of Commerce. Clearly, I was in the best of hands.

Harold is easy going, warm, and dedicated. I'm sure that every one of the many hundreds of college students who have worked for Harold on the Mail Boat or one of the other Gage excursion boats can conjure up the image of Harold, in his khakis and deck shoes, and always in a little bit of a hurry as he marches up and down the Riviera dock with his clipboard.

After meeting Harold, Bill had a surprise for me. I had assumed that there would be some sort of instruction regarding how you jump from a speeding boat onto a pier and back again as fast as you can. But there wasn't. We were going out, and I was just going to do it. Bill had brought along his son, Billy, about seven at the time, and a photographer.

We all piled onto the *Walworth II* and headed out on the lake.

We were taking publicity shots.

I didn't even know if I could really do this.

The pier Bill chose for the photos, and for my first-ever jump as the Mail Girl, was my own pier. (I told you it was the easiest pier to jump). It provided more than enough room for the photographer to set up his camera, and for me to make several jumps without running into him. I also suppose Bill assumed he wouldn't have to explain to the pier owner what we were doing.

I will never forget my first jump. There we were, on my pier, with the very distracting photographer snapping away; and Bill, Billy, Harold, and Neill Frame, the captain, shouting encouragement.

Jumping off wasn't very hard. The forward progress of the boat propelled me, providing plenty of momentum to reach the pier and keep me going toward the mailbox. This is a good thing on most piers (although the Mail Boy had to jump backward, in the opposite direction the boat was travelling, at my old pier at 668 which was part of what made it such a difficult delivery).

But, don't think it was a cake-walk! Standing on the *Walworth II's* rub rail as we came bearing down on the pier, I definitely had an "Oh, my gosh" (or something less printable) moment. The captain must drive fast enough to ensure that the *Walworth II* doesn't drift into the pier, *and* he has to pass close to the pier, but with enough space to ensure that the boat won't hit the pier as it passes—that would definitely throw the Mail Jumper off!

Therefore, there's usually between four and eight feet of churning water that needs to be jumped over at every pier.

Mail Jumpers learn quickly not to look at the water between the boat and the pier. Eyes always need to be on the place you are headed to—whether it's the pier, the mailbox, or the boat. Every jump is unique—adjustments have to be made for each pier, as well as the weather, the amount of mail and whatever else might come into play that day. Someone may have left a raft on the pier right where you would normally land, forcing the Jumper to come up with a quick Plan B. If it's windy, the captain may have to drive by farther away from the pier than normal, or at faster speed. Jumping never become rote, and driving the Mail Boat takes a great deal of skill as well. Maintaining an even speed, getting as close as possible, but not too close, and accounting for wind, waves, rain, and other boats keeps the captain on constant alert.

Yes, jumping off the boat onto the pier for the first time went pretty well. But that was only the first step in the process.

As soon as I landed on the pier, I was moving fluidly. And after the hundreds of times I'd watched the Mail Boy, I knew exactly what to do. A half-dozen fast strides to the mailbox. Open the mailbox door. Slip my handful of letters in. Slam the mailbox door closed.

So far so good.

Now turn back toward the boat.

The *Walworth II* was still there, moving (I'm sure more slowly than normal) past the pier. I reached out with both hands—arms fully extended—and jumped straight at the boat.

This, it turns out, was not correct.

I slammed into the side of the boat. It was sort of a "thunk" experience, completely lacking in grace. However, like many Mail Jumpers before and after me, I was just happy to be back on the boat in one piece.

I had done it. I really was the Mail Jumper!

We circled back around, and I did it again. And again. And again. All the while, the photographer snapped away. Most of the pictures were "action" photos, but for a few, I posed. The most memorable publicity picture taken that day—of me poised, mail in hand with the mailbox door ajar as I delivered mail to myself on my own pier—has graced newspaper articles, a few books, YouTube postings, television shows, and the wall of Pier 290 Restaurant in Williams Bay.

About two hours later, practice was over. The next time I would jump, on the fifteenth of June, it would be for real.

MAIL AND NEWSPAPERS

The Mail Jumper's day doesn't start with the first jump. It starts at seven o'clock every morning at the US Post Office in Lake Geneva which is located at the corner of Main and Center Streets. The first order of business is sorting the mail into cubbies organized for water delivery. This includes newspapers, magazines, packages, and anything else that is normally delivered by the US Postal Service.

After the Mail Jumper sorts, rolls, and rubber-bands the mail by pier, she loads it into a blue cart, and pushes the cart from the post office down to the Riviera dock and the *Walworth II*. When I delivered the mail, I used a plywood box with a lid, a serviceable metal handle, four grocery cart wheels hammered onto the bottom, and a US Post Office logo slapped onto two sides. The mail cart looks pretty much the same today.

Every morning, I loaded up the mail cart, and wheeled it the four blocks to the Riviera. Then I moved the mail from the cart to the *Walworth II*. The bundled mail and newspapers had to be set in the correct order on the shelves so that every delivery is correct. There isn't much time during the mail run to check that you grab the right mail before jumping off the boat, so sorting and stacking the mail before passengers arrive is important. This was, and still is, the schedule Monday through Saturday. On Sunday, since there is no mail, the day starts a little later, and only newspapers are delivered.

Once the mail was ready to go, my job was to help greet the day's passengers, take tickets, and get everyone settled in their seats for the on-time, ten o'clock departure.

The other essential part of the job was learning the scripted story of the history of Lake Geneva and the famous houses, camps, and communities along its shore. In the summer of 1974, the script had just been lovingly expanded, and updated, by Maggie Gage, who along with Ann Wolfmeyer, published *Lake Geneva Newport of the West, 1870-1920*, two years later. The research they did for their book provided an expanded history of the mansions around the lake and the families who had lived in them. The entire excursion boat crew is required to commit the annually-updated script to memory.

I've always loved history, particularly historical biographies, so learning new facts and stories about the houses on the lake was another aspect of the job that I loved. In the 1990s, my love of history and people was put to use when I wrote three historical romance novels. Throughout high school and college, Nancy and I read every historical romance we could get our hands on. Our favorite was, *Shaunna*, written by Kathleen E. Woodiwiss, and in an on-going tradition, cards and emails between us occasionally come from *Shanna*, whose "sensuous, free spirit" we always related to.

But I digress.

As I mentioned, the last half of my first jump was not executed correctly. That fact became immediately clear to me when I landed. Because I was aiming straight at the boat, I smacked into the *Walworth II* like a gnat against a moving windshield. And it hurt. But I learned quickly, as all Mail Jumpers do.

The Mail Jumper always needs to move with the boat. When she jumps off onto the pier, it's at an angle, so that she is pushing off in the same direction that the boat is moving. Jumping back on is the same premise. You must jump at an angle, in the same direction that the boat is going. There is a hand rail that runs the length of the starboard side of the *Walworth II* specifically installed for the Mail Jumpers to hold onto. The fifteen-inch-wide rub rail is used by the Jumpers as a launch-and-landing pad, as well as a walkway.

Within a few days of the first official Mail Boat run, I was moving smoothly from boat to pier and back again as though I'd been doing it all my life. The entire process, when things are working smoothly, is almost like a dance. It goes like this.

Announce the stories of the upcoming houses to the day's passengers, then hand the microphone to the captain (who often times will elaborate or otherwise entertain the passengers, sometimes at the Mail Jumper's expense). Pick up the banded mail for the upcoming pier. Move to the open window of the *Walworth II* just behind the captain's chair. Grab the Mail Jumper rod and swing through the window. Settle both feet on the rub rail, holding the mail in your right hand, while you hold onto the Mail Jumper rod with your left hand. As the boat pulls even with the pier—jump—moving swiftly, and smoothly, to the mailbox. Then turn, run, and leap. The landing is smooth, seamless, and feels great. Now, walk up the side of the boat, swing through the window, and you are ready for the next delivery or to resume the script.

There are between fifty and seventy water deliveries per day on the lake. The number varies from year to year as homes change hands, but some piers have been receiving marine mail for decades. On Sundays, because only newspapers are delivered, there are fewer jumps.

The *Walworth II* always pulled into the Riviera right on schedule at twelve-thirty. When the passengers had been helped off the boat, there was clean up, and prep for the next tour. Although, not the Mail tour, the *Walworth II* runs excursions throughout the day, every day.

With my first jumps completed, life as the Mail Girl settled into as much of a routine as it can be when you jump off of a moving boat for a living.

Mail Girl in Action

Rick Snidtker was the first captain I worked with on the *Walworth II*. Rick was twenty-one to my eighteen and a Summer person. His grandfather had built their cottage in Williams Bay sometime around 1904 and, like so many Lake Geneva families, the Snidtkers were still coming to their summer home seventy years later.

Rick reminded me of the Beach Boys with his blonde hair and easy smile, the requisite well-worn Top-siders, and an incredibly easy-going attitude. He had named the two 5208 Horse Power diesel engines that propelled the *Walworth II*. The engine on the port side he called "Poopsie." "Sugar" was the starboard engine.

When I arrived every morning at eight with the mail cart, he was always there. Often I would find him down in the bilge checking on "the girls." Other times, I would arrive to find Rick nowhere in sight, only to hear him bubble up in a mask and fins from under the hull of the *Walworth II*. I wasn't always sure what he was doing down there—checking on the propellers or looking for I-don't-know-what on the lake bottom. Regardless, he would break the surface of the lake, grab hold of the boat's rub rail, rip off his mask, and shoot me a big grin.

Rick loved the water like nobody else, which is saying a lot, because in Lake Geneva, everyone loves the water. He was attending Florida Atlantic University in Boca Raton Florida and studying marine biology. We used to get into robust discussions about our colleges and their benefits/detractions. It was always FAU versus CU, or vice versa, even though the two universities had almost nothing in common. College-age fisticuffs.

Rick had already worked for Gage Marine for a few summers when he captained the Mail Boat for me. He had even been the Mail Jumper a few years before. Rick taught me a lot about entertaining the passengers. He knew how to charm them with the special stories he would add to the standard script—sometimes it was legends about a mansion and its history, other times, it was recent happenings that he shared. It gave the tour a unique spark, and the audience loved hearing his tidbits.

We got along wonderfully, sharing jokes and trading stories about our nights out in Lake Geneva. It made my already-great summer even more fun. It was the perfect job—I was jumping the mail, I was outside out on the lake all day long, and I had a great captain. I can't think of anything I would have added.

DOGS AND DUCKS

Every summer there are a few animals involved in delivering the mail. That summer there was Nicky, an Alaskan Malamute, and a tame duck at College Camp.

Nicky lived at the Wrigley Boat House and her owners had trained her to fetch the newspaper. Of course, collecting the newspaper from my outstretched hand as we sped by was far more daunting than going to pick up a paper laying immobile on the driveway. Her owners had actually called Lake Geneva Cruise Line to discuss her training. We all worked together to make the paper delivery a success.

I would sit on the transom with a leg wrapped around the window ledge, as I leaned out to position the paper for Nicky to take. Most of the time she did a wonderful job, and once she had the paper she would bound down the pier to the house, tail wagging. A few times we had mishaps. The Sunday paper, we discovered was too bulky for her, so we stopped delivering it to their pier. But on one or two other occasions, our timing was off and either Nicky or I dropped the mail (never in the water). Nicky was distraught over such failures, infrequent as they were, and it would take several days and lots of encouragement coming from people on the boat, and her owners on the pier, to get her to take the paper again.

The duck was a much more passive participant.

There have been camps on Lake Geneva for as long as there have been mansions, some were established before the first mansion was constructed. Originally, most were properties where campers literally pitched their tents in order to share camaraderie and the natural environment of the lake. Holiday Home, Camp Augustana, and George Williams College Camp were the major camps in the late 1970s and all still exit today. Each camp gives children from disadvantaged backgrounds a chance to enjoy a respite from the city.

At all of the camps on Lake Geneva, mail for the campers was sorted into big mail bags that I handed off to a counselor standing on the pier while enthusiastically screaming campers watched the proceedings. At College Camp, the duck would sit calmly in the arm of the counselor as we rushed by and handed off the mail bag. Sometimes he quacked. The passengers loved it.

BAD WEATHER AND WET PIERS

Most days were idyllic and balmy, but not all of them. On rainy days, my job went from the-most-fun-and-wonderful-job-on-earth to something much less pleasant.

There were warm, light rains. There were cold, heavy rains. And then there were storms—when the rain beat down ferociously and the waves washed up between the planks of the piers. I didn't like any of them.

Even in a light rain, it was harder to jump the mail. Rain got in my eyes, making it difficult to see. A baseball cap was de rigueur on rainy days, but only helped a little. Wet and slippery piers made the job much more difficult, as did a wet rub rail.

In 1974, there weren't any rain jackets lightweight and flexible enough to jump the mail in and simultaneously provide sufficient coverage. I learned quickly that there was no point in wearing long pants for warmth. They just ended up sopping wet and twisted around my legs, which made jumping nearly impossible.

This is what rainy days were like. My wet baseball cap was crammed down as close to my eyebrows as I could get it. Even if it was cold, on rainy days I wore shorts, which were soon soaked from the crotch down. My rain slicker was a bright yellow, oiled-canvas jacket that stopped where my legs started. This prevented interference with jumping or running. It did keep my torso dry, but also added to the water running down my legs. It generally took about twenty minutes in a strong rain for my Top-siders to become soggy to the point of squishing as I ran. My fingers were wet and cold, my nose runny, my legs were stiff and freezing. On the worst days, my teeth chattered and my torso shook with chills. Today there is neoprene and light weight running gear made for the rain. The Mail Jumpers must be more comfortable today in their high-tech rain gear; but they still have to make the jumps in the rain. And I'm betting they still dread it.

Those trips weren't very fun for the passengers either in that era. We could only load people into the lower deck, where they were protected from the elements. We dropped the plastic curtains on the main level of the boat, but, at that time, the Mail Boat wasn't heated, making the ride cold and damp for everyone. Today, the *Walworth II* can be completely enclosed and heated to ensure that passengers have a wonderful trip even on days when the weather is less than perfect.

Normally, we had several rows of seats immediately behind the captain's seat, where I jumped on and off the boat. It provided a very up-close and personal view of the action, and usually those seats were considered the best in the house. But on rainy days, no one could, or would want to, sit there. The captain's side-window, and the window immediately behind, him had to be left completely open so Rick could see the pier and me, and so I could climb out the window to make the jumps, which meant that the entire area behind the captain's chair was slippery and soaking wet.

It was also hard to be a chipper and cheery tour guide when I was frozen, soaked, and worried about surviving the next two and a half hours. I was usually less than my most-engaging self on rainy days.

Occasionally, the weather was so bad that the Mail Boat run was cancelled. The mail, however, still had to be delivered. On those days, Rick and I would load the deliveries onto one of the Gage motor boats and deliver the mail, literally, one pier at a time. We had to pull up to, and dock at, each pier, with Rick holding onto the pier post while I climbed out and shoved the mail into the pier mailbox. But we only had to go to the piers that actually had mail that day, allowing us to cut across wide swaths of the lake between destinations.

But despite the anxiety of jumping on rainy days, I never fell on a pier, or missed a jump, because of the rain.

Fog and Willow Trees

The *Walworth II* has other duties in addition to delivering the mail, and so did I.

After the Mail Run returned at twelve-thirty every day, we cleaned the boat and readied her for the afternoon tours. My day was usually over by four-thirty or five o'clock, leaving enough time to fit in water skiing or tubing before dinner.

In the evening, many, if not all, of the Gage fleet was leased out for private parties. Because I always started at the post office early, I was rarely asked to work parties. But occasionally staffing was short, and I joined the crew on the *Lady of Lake* or one of the other excursion boats.

Usually, party passengers arrived and loaded at the Riv, but if it was more convenient to pick up passengers at one of the other municipal piers on the lake, we were happy to accommodate our clients. The historic excursion boats, the *Louise* and *Polaris*, could pick up guests at private piers as well; but the *Lady* and *Belle* were generally too large.

When we picked up all of the passengers at a location other than the Riviera dock, we would deadhead back to the Riv after the party was over and everyone, except for the crew, had disembarked. This was always something special. Clean up could be taken care of back at the Riv, but for the thirty or so minutes it took to get back, we could enjoy being on the lake in the dead of night.

Late night on the lake is wonderful. Even in the days when I would flee from the stifling heat of our house and sleep on the boat's bench-seat using a jib sail as a light blanket, I loved the peacefulness and beauty of the lake at night. Most summer nights the water is smooth as silk—a wide, glassy highway. It's incredibly quiet. The voices on the shoreline have long ago gone to sleep, and all that's left is the engine's soft purr, and the sound of the water parting as the hull cuts through the night.

Aboard the *Lady* or any of the Gage fleet, we would cruise silently down the center of the lake, taking in the beauty and quiet from the captain's cabin high atop the boat, or leaning over the gunnel.

One night, however, instead of an idyllic cruise, we found ourselves lucky to make it back. We had dropped our guests at the Fontana municipal pier and were headed back to the Riv, which is a straight shot for seven miles down the lake, followed by a dogleg left into Geneva Bay. It should have been simple, but a thick, Wisconsin fog rolled in so quickly that before the Fontana dock was a hundred yards behind us, we couldn't see anything.

To our aft, the Fontana beach and lights from Chuck's and the Abbey were completely enveloped in the fog. We couldn't see anything in front of us. We had shortwave radios connecting us to the Cruise Line offices, but no GPS, or directional system, to tell us where we were on the water. Without it, and without a line of sight, boaters may think they're moving in a straight line, but sometimes it's impossible to know. We checked in with the other excursion boats. They'd all made it back to the Riv before the fog rolled in. We were out alone.

The *Lady* crawled, barely moving forward. The captain had to be very careful about where we were headed, but at the same time, he had to avoid drifting, so he kept the huge boat moving forward. Each of the crew members took lookout positions—one person each to the port and starboard sides of the boat, and another two at the bow. Peering into the fog was like trying to see through pudding; but we tried anyhow, hoping to spot a pier light or any other sign that would tell us where we were. We also strained to listen, trying to confirm—based on the sound of the water—that we were still in the middle of the lake. Our biggest fear wasn't finding our way back, it was that we would inadvertently steer too close to the shore. The shoreline and the first fifty feet of the lake from the water's edge were fraught with danger. The *Lady* could hit a buoyed boat, or a pier. Even worse, we could run aground.

One feature of *The Lady of the Lake*, a replica paddleboat and the largest of the Gage excursion fleet, is a gang plank. One end is attached to the bow, while the other end is hoisted ten feet in the air and six feet forward of the bow. As we crept blindly through the fog, one of our crewmembers climbed up the gang plank on its hoist in order to get as far forward on the boat as possible. Like the rest of us, he strained to see, or hear, anything as we motored forward. Then we heard waves lapping, a sign of potential danger since the *Lady* wasn't going fast enough to create waves of its own. It could only be that we were hearing the water against the shore. And with that, the crew member on the gang plank yelled for the captain to hit hard reverse and turn to starboard.

The captain made the maneuver, which wasn't easy with a boat the size of the *Lady of the Lake*. We held our breath, but there was no crash. A few minutes later, clearly shaken, the crewman came down from the gangplank to join the rest of us. As he'd peered out from the gang plank, the branch of a weeping willow had brushed his face. We were literally feet from running into the shore. A disaster had been averted, which everyone was happy about; but we all agreed that now we also had an idea of where we were—Conference Point.

Conference Point is one of the steepest shoreline areas on the lake, with vertical hillsides that drop straight into the water. Willows are one of the few trees that can cling to the steep hillsides there, which forces them to grow out over the water. The lake stays deep longer here because of the drop off, and the shore is particularly dark because houses are located at the top of the cliffs, not along the shoreline. Thus there were no piers or lights to help us with our way-finding. We had come dangerously close to shore, probably less than ten feet, and if not for the willow leaves brushing across the crewman's head and the captain's quick response, we would certainly have run aground.

I was relieved to have survived that close encounter, but it was disheartening that we weren't even out of Fontana Bay. That meant another hour or two of creeping through the water to reach the Riviera dock. Re-oriented, we continued slowly down the lake. As we moved east the fog lightened. By the time we reached the Narrows, we could make out lights on piers on both shorelines to help us slip safely through the notch. When we rounded into Geneva Bay, I was incredibly glad to see the Riv lights shining through the fog.

Life Guards and Laughter

Mark O'Donoghue and I had continued to date long-distance through my freshman year at CU, while he finished his senior year at Badger High. But, as so often happens in college, three weeks before I left Boulder for the summer, I met someone.

I had decided to get my summer tan started early, but the day wasn't cooperating. It was sunny, but cool, so I donned a bikini, bundled up my beach towel, and headed to CU's Folsom Stadium. I set myself up on the AstroTurf in the southwest corner of the football field, and let the sun shine down. Although I applauded my ingenuity, it was a little strange lying there alone in an empty football stadium. No matter. I closed my eyes, soaked up the sun, and promptly fell asleep.

An hour later, I woke up to someone blocking my "rays." My friend, Don Hasselbeck, had recently moved out of our dorm and into an off-campus apartment. As he came out of the training room at the north end of the field with one of his new roommates, he spotted me—or at least some crazy girl in a bikini—at the far end of the stadium and decided to explore further. When it turned out to be me, we had a short discussion and he introduced me to his roommate, Dave Logan. Saturday night, I ran into Dave again at the Skunk Creek Inn, a local dance club. I was smitten.

Three weeks later when finals were over, I returned to Lake Geneva to take on the Mail Boat, and Dave headed to Europe to play basketball. There was some discussion about Dave coming through Chicago on his way back from Europe in early July. It was a loose plan at best, but I put the entire faith of my eighteen-year-old heart into the belief that he would do everything he could to meet me in Chicago.

Me being me, I returned home and immediately told Mark that I couldn't see him anymore. It was a painful breakup after two years of dating.

It was even worse when I didn't hear much from Europe. But I remained steadfast in my belief in this new relationship, right up to the week of our Chicago rendezvous, which arrived and then passed with nary a word from my new beau.

It was about ten days later that I found myself in the Geldermann kitchen at Edgewood, lamenting the mess I had made of my personal life. Mark wouldn't speak to me, and Dave, well Dave was clearly not my new boyfriend. Nancy, being the exceptional friend she is, reminded me that I was getting a lot of attention from one of the Water Safety Patrol lifeguards working at the Lake Geneva Public Beach, which was located right next to the Riviera dock.

Mike Bona was a summer person, and actually seemed interested in me despite my complete focus on the Chicago rendezvous rather than the cute lifeguard.

Nancy and I decided to change that immediately.

We launched both the Sunfish and a barely-formed plan to sail down to Mike's beach and check him out. As we tacked our way into Lake Geneva Bay, we picked apart my break up with Mark, Dave's no-show status, and the potential of Mike. We arrived at the Riv only to realize that there was really nowhere to dock the Sunfish. So, we decided to take a quick tack past the public beach. Nothing obvious, of course.

As with most of our ill-defined plans, things didn't go the way we'd anticipated. We sailed too close to the shore (wanting to get a *really* good look), lost the wind, and drifted into the *No Boats* zone of the beach. I had to jump in and pull the Sunfish while Nancy frantically pumped the rudder back and forth. Our attempts to get away from the beach finally worked, but the entire time Mike was sitting in the guard chair yelling into the megaphone, "Get the sailboat out of the swim area!"

Our stealth plan was a bust.

On the sail home, we concluded that our motto for the summer would be "Love the One You're With." We sang Stephen Stills' song the entire sail home, and by the end of the summer, Nancy had needlepointed a "Love the One You're With" pillow for me, which I took back to CU and still sits in my bedroom.

Mike and I started dating the next week.

Antics and Engine Troubles

Early in August, I arrived with my trusty mail cart full of mail to discover that Sugar and Poopsie were refusing to fire up. Given all the attention Rick gave those two, I was amazed that they were not better behaved; but boat engines can be fickle. Sugar and Poopsie had decided that, today, they were not in the mood to cooperate. Rick, as well as one of the engine specialists from the Williams Bay boat yard, huddled down in the bilge while I waited on the dock with the day's passengers.

Finally, ten o'clock arrived and everyone had to admit that despite all best efforts, the "girls" would not be running that day. Tickets were refunded with vast apologies by all and the crowds dispersed to other Lake Geneva entertainment, but the mail still had to be delivered.

With our boat out of commission, Rick and I wouldn't have our normal one o'clock and three o'clock excursions either. Harold allocated one of the Gage Whalers for mail delivery and we headed out. It was a glorious late summer morning and about eleven by the time we loaded the mail up and headed out. Just Rick, me, a bench full of rubber banded letters and newspapers, the sun, and the calm, clear lake. Unlike the deliveries we made without the *Walworth II* in downpours, today we were in no rush.

None at all.

We putted along from pier to pier, stopping at the camp piers for long conversations with counselors, and engaging in a lot of waving at kids. We flagged down the Water Safety Patrol for a mid-lake chat, and checked in at a few friends' piers to solidify plans for that night's softball game, and, later, foosball tournaments at Chuck's in Fontana.

Eventually we made it to Black Point.

Black Point is another of the very famous estates on the lake. Built in the 1880s, the house at Black Point is one of the finest examples of Queen Anne architecture in the Midwest and contains one of the most complete collections of Victorian furniture as well. But Black Point is as famous for its property as for its stunning house.

In the 1880s, Conrad Seipp, a German immigrant, purchased twenty-seven acres that included the entire point from the shoreline to the peak of the steep hill that rises from the water's edge. Conrad was the owner of Seipp Brewing Company, which dominated the Chicago beer market in the late 1800s and early twentieth century. Seipp Brewing Company became one of the largest breweries in the United States before closing at the tail end of prohibition.

The Seipps hired Adolph Cudell, who had designed homes for other notables in Chicago including Cyrus McCormick, to design two houses for them. One, their primary residence, was built near the Seipp brewery on the south side of Chicago; the other was their summer home at Black Point.

They located their thirteen-bedroom Lake Geneva home high on the hill where summer breezes would cool the house throughout the day, and expansive views to the lake and across tree tops could be enjoyed from nearly every room.

In the first years after the house was completed, it was only accessible by boat. Family and guests arrived from the city at the Williams Bay depot to be greeted by the Seipp's steamship, the *Loreley*. Once aboard, guests cruised across the lake to the Black Point boat house, located on the western side of the point.

The Seipps added to the original twenty-seven acres by buying various adjoining farms and properties until the estate totaled fifty-three acres, nearly entirely undisturbed. They hired the city of Chicago's Landscape Architect, Olaf Benson, to design the grounds. Over the years, the family added new plantings, until in the 1970s it was widely told that Black Point was home to over sixty different species of evergreen trees alone, one of the most unique, private, collections in America.

Although Conrad Seipp only enjoyed the house and gardens on Black Point for two seasons before his death in 1890, his family and four generations of descendants kept the mansion and property intact, including six hundred and twenty feet of shoreline. In 2005, Seipp's great-grandson, William O. Petersen, donated the house, grounds, and furnishings to the State of Wisconsin as a historic site. Today, Black Point is run by the Wisconsin Historical Society. Black Point Estate and Gardens is open for tours from May through October. Visitors can only reach the site as the family did originally, by boat. Lake Geneva Cruise Line runs special Black Point trips throughout the summer and fall. And, speaking of Lake Geneva Cruise Line…

There we were, bouncing past Black Point in the Whaler with about two-thirds of our deliveries made. We were just thinking that maybe we should finish our route and head back to the Riviera before Harold noticed we'd been gone so long, when our third engine of the day quit on us.

The Whaler's Mercury outboard motor sputtered and died. The bow of the boat sunk slightly in the water as it slowed, and then glided to a stop.

Like Conference Point, Black Point's shoreline is mostly untamed with only a few houses or piers. And, of course, the Water Safety Patrol boat was long gone. It was early in the week, so there weren't many boats out, and the water was as smooth as glass, which meant no breeze and no drift.

Rick checked the gas cans and the fuel hose. He pumped the

gas bulb to prime the engine. The electric starter wasn't doing anything, and we didn't want to flood the engine. We waited a bit, then took turns yanking on the engine's hand pull. Twenty minutes of that wore us out.

We laid back and pondered our dilemma as we bobbed forty feet off of Black Point.

It was hot. We jumped in the lake to cool off. I told Rick stories about Joey Bidwell and me picnicking with the horses on the Black Point beach, which we could see from where we floated. He told me that he wanted to become a deep sea diver.

We finally decided to swim the boat to the nearest pier. As we were executing that plan, the Water Safety Patrol found us. They radioed into their Headquarters Shack at the Riv and notified Harold to send a boat that could tow the Whaler in for repairs. Rick stayed with the Whaler. I got a ride back to the Riv with the Safety Patrol. I have no idea how the rest of the mail got delivered that day. Sugar and Poopsie never gave out again while I jumped the mail.

FAME AND FALLING IN

Harold and his marketing team had put the publicity photos taken on my first jump to good use. They had gone out on the Associated Press (AP) wire along with a press release about the Mail Boat and the first time in sixty-five years that a girl was jumping the mail. The story was incredibly popular. In July and August, stories and photos started showing up everywhere from the *Janesville Gazette* down the road to the *Chicago Daily News*, the *Des Moines Register* and *Detroit News*. It was even published in *Stars and Stripes*, the internationally distributed newspaper of the US Military. A *Wall Street Journal* reporter showed up just before

Labor Day weekend and on the twenty-second of September, the Mail Boat and I were featured on the front page of the *Journal*. The publicity continues today. Lake Geneva's Mail Boat and the Mail Jumpers regularly make national news—in print, on television, and on the internet.

My first summer as the Mail Girl was coming to an end. So, of course, the question that lives in the mind of every Mail Jumper all summer long, was in my mind too.

Will I fall in?

It's the question most asked by guests on the Mail Route. Trust me, Mail Jumpers do no want to miss the boat and fall in unexpectedly. There are two very big propellers churning the water at the back of the *Walworth II*, and no one wants to be in the water anywhere near them when they are running.

But every Mail Jumper, no matter how deeply grateful that they've never fallen in, also secretly wonders... what would it be like? What would happen if I did fall in?

And so the day came when I decide to miss the boat on purpose.

Rick and I had discussed this at length. Which pier would work the best? We wanted to give the passengers a show; but we also wanted to get me out of the water quickly, the *Walworth II* turned around easily, and continue on our route efficiently. Picking the right pier was essential.

I wanted a hot, calm day so that jumping in the lake was as refreshing and enjoyable as possible. I also wanted to drip-dry quickly.

I don't think we fooled anyone onboard on "The Day". I missed by a lot, which was all about landing in the water as far from both the propeller churn and the pull of boat's draft as possible, while still looking at least a little as though I had tried to get back on the boat. The crowd was thrilled with our antics and I got a few hugs from passengers when everyone disembarked at the end of the tour. It was fun. A rite of passage as a Mail Jumper, and a chance to ham it up for our guests.

The next summer, I really did almost fall in, and that was an experience that still puts my heart into my throat.

Mail Girl Redux

After finishing my sophomore year at CU, I was back in Lake Geneva again, and couldn't wait to jump the mail. This summer there were no unknowns. I knew exactly how my summer would go, and I was in a rush to get to it.

Rick didn't return to Gage Marine. We had become pen pals during the school year, writing infrequent, but long, letters to each other. We would continue our letter writing for many years. After college, Rick went to California where he obtained his commercial diving certification. He became a diver for the oil industry, and twice I received letters from him while he was in a decompression chamber in the North Sea after being underwater for several weeks. His family still owns their summer cottage in Williams Bay.

The summer of 1975, my captain was Neill Frame. He was a great captain and, as of 2014, Neill is still the captain of the Mail Boat. Like Rick, he is a wonderful story-teller and charms the Mail Boat audiences. Neill also gives advice to the college students trying out for the Mail Jumper position.

That summer was nothing short of wonderful. In my

sophomore year as the Mail Girl, I wasn't worried about having to learn something new, or make mistakes. I had the enthusiasm of a nineteen-year-old and the confidence of an old hand. As with every Lake Geneva summer, each day was special. Some days I rode my bike to work. Sometimes I went water skiing at six in the morning and had my water skiing partners drop me at the Riviera dock by seven-thirty. I'd run into the Riv ladies bathroom to change into my red, white and blue, and then head up the street to the post office.

My circle of friends expanded geometrically and in every direction that summer. Somehow, although all of us had been at Lake Geneva all summer for most of our lives; it was only when we returned to the lake for college summers that we came together. I think we collided somewhere at the intersection of sun, and water, and being young. It was as if someone had tossed us together like a salad, and the blending was amazing. My friends became a delicious mix of summer people, high school friends, and locals from the other area high schools in Fontana and Williams Bay.

I found new friends and old ones, reconnected with childhood acquaintances, and became fast friends with people whose names I'd only heard of during high school. Nancy developed a crush on the lifeguard at Fontana Beach who turned out to be my winter-time kindergarten buddy from River Forest. I even crossed paths again with Ann Herring, my best friend at age four.

Mike and I had continued to date through the winter, and when summer returned, we went back to being the lifeguard and the Mail Girl. On our days off, we waterskied and tubed with friends, many of whom were on the Water Safety Patrol with Mike. We met other boats at Conference Point and dropped anchor to swim, hang out in floating lounge chairs, and do backflips off the tree swing into the lake. Several nights a week, like almost everyone else, we went to Chuck's. Whenever possible, we went by boat.

One hot night in August, Mike and I were making a slow, late-night cruise back to my house when the aurora borealis began streaking the sky with incredible columns of green and white light. The lake was deadly calm, and the luminous light show wasn't just overhead—it was reflected in the water all around us, creating another magical night on the lake.

HAM SANDWICHES AND HOBIE CATS

On days that I waterskied before work, I often didn't have time to make a lunch, so I got into the habit of calling home before the Mail Boat departed at ten to give my brother, Andrew, instructions for making me a sandwich. Generally, I was a fan of ham and cheese with a little mustard. Andrew would come down to the pier when Neill and I came by on the Mail Boat and switch out the brown bag lunch he'd made me for the mail I handed him. Most days I ate the sandwich long before we made it back to the Riviera because after water skiing and jumping the mail, I was starving long before the mail tour was over at twelve-thirty.

I still loved to sail, but the M-20 required more concentration than I was willing to invest, and the Sunfish was a little boring. I found the answer with one of my best friends, Kevin Forbeck. His father, George Forbeck, was Tom Geldermann's partner at Geldermann and Company, and one of the most significant independent corn brokers at the Chicago Board of Trade. He was married to my former neighbor on the south shore, Jennifer Kinzer. They owned a lakefront home, Deepwood, on Fontana's north shore.

As with the Geldermanns, I gravitated toward the Forbecks,

and their big, welcoming family as well as the three boys Kevin, Michael, and Vance. Throughout college, I spent a lot of time in the Forbeck kitchen, or down at their pier, listening to stories about big corn trades with China, and Jennifer's efforts to set up technology systems in third world countries.

The Forbecks had a Hobie Cat, a catamaran sailboat that was fairly new in the sailing world. The Hobie-16 has a pair of lightweight, fiberglass hulls, two sails, and dual trapeze rigs. Kevin and I spent many afternoons racing back and forth across Fontana Bay, one hull smacking through the waves while the two of us hiked as far out on the windward hull as we could get. Flipping was part of the catch-your-breath fun of the Hobie Cat, and there were plenty of times when Kevin pushed the boat to its limits, and I ended up airborne in the trapeze as we summersaulted the Hobie into the lake.

As much as I liked sailing, skiing, tubing, and boating, I loved the end of each of those days equally. The boats were up on their hoists. I was tired, but in a wonderfully physical way. My skin was warm, and a little bit sunburnt, and my hair was a mess of streaky blonde strands that stuck to my face and neck. I felt like a wildcat strolling slowly across the lawn while the golden sun sank toward the horizon and the lake glittered as though a million diamonds floated on its surface.

Maple Trees and Halter Tops

Possibly, the most unique mail jump delivery is along the south shore between the Lake Geneva Yacht Club and Black Point. Similar to the row of deliveries that the Mail Boy had to make near my family's pier at 668, this is a series of five, adjacent piers, all of which receive marine delivery. What makes this such a special series of piers is that the shape of the shoreline and the lake bottom makes it impossible for the *Walworth II* to run alongside each pier for delivery. The answer to the problem has always been simple— the Mail Jumper simply delivers the mail along the shoreline.

At the first pier, the Mail Jumper leaps off the boat with the mail for all five piers. Delivery at the first pier is standard—put the mail in the mailbox nailed to one of the pier posts. But then it's a mad sprint down the pier to the shore. The next three mailboxes are on the shoreline next to each pier. It's a crazy run across the uneven front lawns while jumping over tree roots, and dodging balls and sand toys left out overnight. Then it's a rattling race down the last pier to the final mailbox and—hopefully—a leap that reconnects the Jumper with the boat. While all of this is going on, Neill narrates this unique set of deliveries.

While it might seems that boat and Jumper are disconnected during this sprint along the shoreline, it's very much the opposite. The captain has to carefully gage his speed while the Jumper is running the route, so that both Jumper and boat arrive at the fifth pier at the same time. When it works, and most of the time it is an incredibly well-synchronized dance, the *Walworth II* glides by just as the Jumper slams the door on the last mailbox, then pivots, and leaps onto the back of the boat. Tah-dah!

There were, however, a few mishaps for me during my shore runs. Twice I was too slow (or the boat was too fast) and Neill had to reverse engines to slow down enough for me to make it back on board

Another time, Neill had to circle around and make a second pass at the pier in order for me to jump on.

But this was not entirely my fault.

It was a perfect July day, hot and breezeless, without a cloud in the sky. I had dressed accordingly in white shorts, a red, white, and blue halter-top, pony-tail, and plenty of sunscreen. Things were going perfectly as I landed on the first pier, made my delivery, and headed for the shore. I rounded onto the grass, and was headed for the next mailbox when the button holding my halter-top together popped off.

This is what people saw from the *Walworth II*: the Mail Girl running down the pier. The Mail Girl running along the shore. The Mail Girl passing behind a very large Maple. And… nothing. Where was the Mail Girl?

Neill was wondering the same thing, because no one could see me behind the big, black trunk of that tree. And thank goodness, because that is where I had to stop and come up with a very quick fix. I did the only thing there was to do. I tied the two ends of my top together behind my neck. I emerged from behind my tree—trying to act as though nothing had happened—running for my life. I had the rest of the mail deliveries in-hand, but my cute, nautical, halter top now looked more like a baby bib strangling me under my chin.

Of course, because of my wardrobe malfunction, I was far behind the *Walworth II*, and Neill had to circle back to the last pier so I could jump on. Between Neill's questioning look and the curiosity of the passengers, I knew this was no time to be demure. I just took the microphone and explained what had happened. I got a good chuckle from our audience.

I never wore a halter-top to jump the mail again.

This story brings up an obvious, but important, fact worth pointing out. There is no other way for the Mail Jumper to get back on the boat except to jump. There was never a time that I could just step back onto the *Walworth II*. No time that it was just waiting for me. It's jump or get left behind. And you can't get left behind. What happens to the rest of the deliveries? What happens to the tour? And, how do you get back to the Riviera? I'd already completed my fair share of walks around the lake as a ten year old; it was not something I felt the need to repeat, especially not because I'd missed the boat (so to speak).

Jump is the only option. So jump the Jumpers do.

A NEAR MISS AND A LITTLE BOY'S RESCUE

Remember my fake "miss" last summer? That is the fun way to take a fall, but I never wanted to unexpectedly end up in the water behind the transom of the *Walworth II*. Especially on rainy days, I was hyper-aware of the nasty, churning waters just aft of the stern.

But the scariest day I had as the Mail Jumper was not a rainy day. It was cold and blustery, but the boat and the pier were dry. I was just finishing the South Shore Five, running in my wind breaker and shorts down the last pier. I got the mail into the box and turned. The *Walworth II* was moving faster than I'd anticipated, and my only option was was to jump onto the very back of the boat.

The Jumper rub rail runs the entire length of the boat; but the grab bar ended about three-quarters of the way down the boat and well before this back section. At that time, passengers who sat in this area were out in the open, similar to those on the upper deck. There was a perforated metal screen that ended at about the passenger's chest level, which was at about my eye level if I was standing on the rub rail.

I knew I was late on my jump, but it wasn't the first time I'd jumped for the back of the boat. The difference was that I was cold, and my muscles and hands were stiff.

I jumped. But I was so late that I ended up jumping straight at the boat instead of with it. I hit the metal siding hard. I grabbed the top of the back screen with my left hand, but my feet missed the rub rail completely. My shins slammed against edge of the rail. I had mail in my right hand which I should have dropped, but my mail jumping instinct kicked in, and I held onto the out-going mail. The boat continued to move. Neill could only assume that I was on board and fine. I scrambled to get my feet up on the rub rail, but before I could get my footing, I felt the palm of my hand slipping on the cold metal railing.

I was going to fall.

Images of the churning diesel propellers flashed through my mind. And then, a boy, about ten-years-old, who was sitting in the seat next to the rail, jumped up and clamped his hand hard over mine, and held on. It was enough for me to get my feet onto the rub rail and pull myself up. He was just tall enough for his head to be level with mine over the top of the metal panel. Our noses were about eight inches apart as I thanked him. I had never meant it more.

There wasn't time to do more than gather my wits and head down the rub rail to the front of the boat. My heart was still in my throat, but I grabbed the microphone and again thanked "the boy in the back who grabbed my hand." I absolutely believe that, if not for him, I would have slid down the slide of the boat, and fallen into the wake of the Mail Boat.

Water Girl

W hen Labor Day arrived, I knew in my heart that my Mail Jumping days were coming to a close. I loved jumping the mail just as much as I'd known I would; but I saw other experiences out there yet to be lived

In many ways, I knew that my balmy, idyllic, summers would soon come to an end; that, too soon, it would be time to walk away from my magical days of summer fun, and focus on more substantial things. Soon I would have to become an adult. But I had two summers left, and they needed to be on the lake.

I approached Dick Scherff, the Director of Lake Geneva's Water Safety Patrol about a job. The Patrol's headquarters is located on the Riviera dock about thirty feet from Lake Geneva Cruise Line's ticket booth, and during my two years jumping mail, I had spent many of my lunch breaks in the Patrol Shack chatting with Dick and Mary Pat Genoar, who ran the shortwave radio communications for the Patrol around the lake.

The Water Safety Patrol was established by Simeon Chapin in 1920. It started out as a small group dedicated to promoting lake safety including swimming, sailing, and motor boating. The first efforts were posters and bulletins posted at area beaches, but soon the Patrol began hiring swimming instructors and offering free lessons at various locations around the lake. By 1925, the Patrol was also providing lifeguards at many of the municipal beaches. That same year, the organization expanded its services with the purchase of its first Patrol boat, which provided rescue services and assistance to distressed boaters on the lake.

Dick had been the Director since I was about three years old, and had built the Patrol to a team of more than forty life guards, swimming instructors, and boat crew. Mary Pat was giving up her position, and I wanted to take over after she left. Dick agreed. So I left for Colorado knowing that the next summer would again bring new experiences.

New Houses and Travel Adventures

The next twelve months turned out to bring more new experiences than I could have imaged. Just before I arrived home for Christmas break, I learned that we were moving to Ceylon Point, which has a very well-known history on the lake.

Ceylon Point occupies the south point where Geneva Bay ends. It is a high ridge that drops steeply to the water and has an uninterrupted view of the entire length of the lake. Just past the point, the land flattens and the shoreline curves softly into Buttons Bay.

The first home to occupy the site was brought to the lake in 1894 in twenty-one box cars by real estate mogul Frank R. Chandler. A year earlier, Chicago had hosted the Columbian Exposition (the Chicago World's Fair) which had a lasting effect on architecture, sanitation, the arts, and American optimism. For the fair, Queen

Victoria commissioned a tea house, designed as a reproduction of a Buddhist temple to promote Ceylonese tea and Ceylon (now Sri Lanka), a British protectorate. The building was assembled by native craftsmen brought to the Chicago fairgrounds to build it. It was constructed using nineteen different types of wood native to Ceylon and wooden pegs rather than nails.

When the Exposition ended, the Chandlers bought the building and moved it their newly purchased property on the point. Immediately after the Ceylon Court tea house was sited on the point at Lake Geneva, the Chandler's hired architect Henry Lord Gay to expand the building and turn it into their summer home. The Chandler's insisted that the addition match the original building in materials as well as construction methodology.

The Chandlers sold Ceylon Court to John J. Mitchell in 1901. Mitchell had been named President of Illinois Merchants Trust Company (later Continental Illinois Bank) at the age of twenty-seven and later became its Chairman. In addition to the house, the Mitchell's owned the steamship *Louise*, which still gives steam-driven tours around the lake as part of the Lake Geneva Cruise Line fleet.

The Mitchells had five children. Their oldest son, John J. Mitchell Jr., married Lolita Armour of the Chicago meatpacking family in 1920. For many years, they were considered the wealthiest couple in America with combined fortunes of more than one hundred and twenty million dollars.

In 1927, the senior Mitchell and his wife were killed while driving in an open car from Lake Geneva to Chicago for a funeral.

After the Mitchells' untimely death, washing machine manufacturer F. L. Maytag purchased Ceylon Court. The Maytag's summered in the house until 1948 when the point was subdivided. The Ceylonese house was razed in 1958, and shortly thereafter, another large home was built on the eastern edge of the point with a broad lawn that reached across the point and offered uninterrupted views across the lake. The house, now named Ceylon Point, was white brick with a gray slate roof, a similarly-styled gatehouse, and boathouse, seven hundred and twenty feet of lakefront, and ten acres of land.

We moved in just after Christmas, while I was still on my semester break. The entrance to Ceylon Point is through twin white-brick pillars and a wrought iron gate on Lake Shore Drive just east of Button's Bay. From the road, you can see the gatehouse which has a four-car garage and a pair of two-bedroom apartments on the second story.

Like Tanglewood, Ceylon Point had tennis courts and a pool, but everything about this house was taken to a higher level. The bedroom Alexa and I moved into was on the back of the house, and although our bedroom view of the lake was gone, we had a beautiful bay window that looked out over a fountain and across the wooded acres behind the house. Ceylon Point was full of burnished, dark wood floors and beautiful antique brass chandeliers. The kitchen still had its original icebox, and a wonderful white-enamel gas oven, with a six-burner stove and warming drawer, that cooked better than any oven I've used before or since.

My favorite part of the house was the family room that looked out over a big, wood deck and across the lake. From the floor-to-ceiling wall of windows, I could see all the way to Fontana. In the summer, the sun sparkled across the water all afternoon; in the winter, red sunsets shone through the rising steam as the annual thick cover of ice formed. In the spring, the nights reverberated with the boom of ice breaking up, and the promise of the summer to come.

The trip from the house to the pier was down a long, winding flagstone path and staircase that followed the original house's walkway. At the water's edge, there was a boathouse with a one bedroom apartment and patio. The pier had three boat slips.

I barely had time to get settled into Ceylon Point, because, at the end of January, I was taking a semester off to travel around the world with my parents and brother. In four month, we visited fifteen countries, including New Zealand, Indonesia, Nepal, India, Kenya and Brazil. Apartheid was still the order of the day when we arrived in South Africa, and civil war was underway in Rhodesia (now Zimbabwe). It was an entirely rare and life-changing voyage that altered how I saw the world and humanity forever. But by early May, I was back home in Lake Geneva.

Radios and Kissing Skis

The house at Ceylon Point didn't have a pier mailbox. Our land mailbox was close to the house, and easier to access than the pier; making it less convenient to get mail by water. But my life was still connected to the Mail Boat.

Nancy replaced me as the Mail Jumper that summer, and, over the next several years, she would be followed by four of her siblings—Tom, Elyse, Stephen, and Bob. I was very happy to see Gage continue to hire girls to jump the mail. It was amazing to me that my dream as a six-year-old had become more than just my own reality; it had created permanent change. There would never be only Mail Boys again.

Working at the Patrol Shack was as different from jumping the mail as it was similar. I still waterskied to work several days a week, I was outside all day long, and I was lake-side. But at the Shack I was primarily sitting, not jumping. I was responsible for keeping track of the Patrol boats and lifeguards at each of the beaches. Everyone communicated by short wave radio and it was my job to log all transmissions.

Most days communications were mundane—a *ten-eight* from each guard as they checked in for duty, followed by an off duty *ten-seven* during their lunch hour and at the end of the day. Boat crews regularly reported their *twenty* so I always had a record of their location. I also issued *ten-nineteens* to call a boat back to the Shack when Dick requested.

The boat crews handled everything from stranded boats to significant accidents. They were also the only system for getting boaters off the lake when bad weather threatened.

On the lake, the day can go from sunny and calm to thunder and lightning, five foot waves, and thirty mile-an-hour wind gusts in a matter of minutes; so when we received a weather alert or could see a storm coming from the west, I would call all boats and guards with a *ten-thirteen* weather update. The boat crews would immediately set up the big red storm flag on the engine box and circle the shoreline while they boomed a warning from their megaphones, while the lifeguards at every beach would get all swimmers out of the water until the danger had passed.

Although most days were relaxed and easy, we all knew that an emergency could occur at any time. I dreaded the thought of a *ten-fifty* call coming from a beach or boat, messaging that a serious, potentially fatal, accident had occurred.

One time a very frantic father came tearing into the Shack because he'd lost his daughter. Anyone who lives on the lake understands that as wonderful as the water is, it is also a danger. He was terrified by the possibility that his child had fallen under the Riviera dock. In less than a minute, we had crew members in the water with snorkels and masks searching for the missing three year old, while I searched through the crowds in the Riviera building and on the docks. Fortunately, she was found safe and on dry land in the Riviera Arcade.

During my two summers working in the Patrol Shack, we never had a drowning or death, but accidents have always occurred on the lake. Newspaper accounts of drownings go back as far as the 1880s. In 1895, there was a particularly unfortunate event in which six people drowned when their thirty-foot steam launch, *Dispatch*, capsized on a Sunday when a storm swept in suddenly in the late afternoon.

Today the Water Safety Patrol has six boats, provides lifeguards at a dozen beaches around the lake, offers swimming lessons, boat safety classes, and lifeguard training, and employs a staff of over eighty people. It is funded almost entirely by private donations and has received national recognition for excellence from both the American Red Cross and the National Safety Council.

The major fundraising event for the Patrol is always the August Dinner Dance. Supporters from around the lake join the Patrol staff and Board of Directors to hear about the year's achievements and celebrate another year of the Patrol working to keep the lake safe.

The week before the dance that summer, Dick asked me if I would join him on stage to help with the silent auction announcements and drawings. I was honored and excited. Then three days before the dance I was getting in an hour of skiing before work, with Mike and Tom Polek, when I had my first, and only, water skiing accident.

We were skiing just off of Button's Bay, not far from my house. I was skiing and took a fall (which happened constantly to me). But this time, when I fell, I went forward as my ski flew up and backward. My face and the edge of my O'Brien slalom ski collided.

I was conscious, but definitely knocked a little loopy. As the boat circled around to pick me up, I focused on putting my head back and relaxing in the water, letting my life vest do its job.

Mike and Tom knew that something had happened, but it wasn't until they helped me climb into the boat that they could see my scraped up face and bloody nose. They were both on the Patrol boat crew, so once I was back in the boat, we headed straight to the Patrol Shack where they raided the first aid kit for an ice pack, dabbed Bacitracin on my wounds, and helped me pack my left nostril with cotton and Kleenex (ick). Then they took off for the first boat shift.

Once I assured him I was fine, Dick just chuckled at me.

I worked all day, continuously changing out my nose-packing materials. By the end of the day, my nose was still bleeding and the ice pack hadn't alleviated how much the left side of my face hurt (and yes, there were plenty of "But it's killing me" jokes). So I headed to the hospital to have it checked out. A panel of X-rays showed that I'd fractured my check bone, but, somehow, that sounded better to me than a broken nose. There was nothing that could be done for the fracture, except to let it heal.

Three days later, I was up on the dinner dance stage with Dick, sporting a pattern of scabs running from my left eyebrow to just below my left nostril. Dick made sure to point that out to everyone, explaining that I had gotten too friendly with my ski and decided to "kiss" it.

More Mail Jumpers

During the 1980s, Lake Geneva Cruise Line expanded the *Walworth II*, cutting through the center of the boat width-wise and adding ten feet to its length. The expansion enabled them to add more seating for passengers and a significant amount of additional real estate to the rub rail, giving the Jumpers a little more time and space to get back on the boat.

In 1989, Lake Geneva Cruise Line began hiring between five and six Jumpers every summer—usually three are assigned as regulars for the job of Mail Jumper while the others become alternates. That program is still in place today. Having more Jumpers in the schedule allows everyone the flexibility to take days off as needed for family events. They also started holding formal tryouts for the job. Tryouts are held on the Thursday before Mail Boat deliveries begin on the fifteenth of June. Which means, by the way, that Mail Jumpers still don't get much practice before real mail jumping starts.

Candidates are judged on both their ability to jump, as well as how engaging and polished they can be while giving the scripted tour. The panel of judges, includes Harold Friestad, other Gage Marine management personnel, and a few Jumpers from past years. About twelve to fifteen people try out annually. Harold assures me that they get "rock stars" every year.

In 2004, the *Walworth II* went through a major facelift. The back and upper decks were enclosed, permanent, operable windows were added on all levels, mahogany trim was installed, and she got a new, navy paint job. Cameras were mounted on the starboard side of the boat and monitors added on the port side, so that every passenger has a great view of the jumper as he makes deliveries. She emerged a very refined ship—now much more Princess Fiona than Shrek.

Because there are so many new, large mansions being built on the lake, the tour now includes a great deal of information on current owners and the architectural features of many of the newer estates. The tour also now includes pictures of the historic homes as they were originally built. These are displayed on the monitors as the tour progresses past those sites.

In 2014, the *Walworth II* once again went through a major restoration.

Today, the Jumpers wear a uniform of red polo shirts and shorts. They also wear an uninflated life vest as an added safety feature. The fame of the US Mail Boat and the story of jumping the mail on Lake Geneva continues. Year after year, newspapers, magazines, and news stations across the United States, and beyond, chronicle the story. In recent years, CNBC and CBS Sunday Morning have filmed segments aboard the *Walworth II*.

Today, if you bring a stamped letter, or postcard, with you for your ride aboard the US Mail Boat, you can have it hand-cancelled with a one-of-a-kind Mail Boat stamp. In 2012, Nancy's daughter, Annie Williams, had the invitations for her wedding hand-cancelled with the Mail Boat stamp, a special recognition of her own recent history as a Lake Geneva Mail Girl.

In 2016, marine delivery on Lake Geneva will celebrate its one hundredth year of continuous service.

I loved jumping the mail—the passengers, the stories about the homes, and being out on the water all day, every day. Even more, I loved the sun, the wind, and the sense of flight that jumping gave me. I also loved working for the Water Safety Patrol. I am very proud to have been a part of two organizations so vital to the story of the lake.

Most of all, I loved life on Lake Geneva. Flying over the lake's rough chop in the boat; diving into the sweet, clear water on a hot afternoon; cruising aimlessly down the center of the lake in the post-midnight calm. It was all as good as it gets.

But life had other plans for me.

Sunset Girl

The summer of 1976, I returned to the Patrol Shack, water skiing, softball games, nights at Chuck's, and the wonders of summer in Lake Geneva. By August, Mike and I had broken up, and I was headed toward graduation from CU in December. Although I didn't realize it then, that summer would be my last in Lake Geneva.

After graduation, I did a brief stint in Los Angeles working for Merrill Lynch on Hollywood Boulevard. Six months of that was enough for me. In November, I transferred with Merrill to Chicago and a position working on the Options Exchange at the Board of Trade. Nancy was trading corn on the Board and living in Chicago, as were Kevin and Michael Forbeck, and several other friends from the lake. My position was significantly less glamorous than theirs, as they were all either trading or working as brokers in various Board of Trade "pits." I was working in Merrill's operations group and held various jobs over the next seven months; by May, my natural impatience had kicked in, and I knew I was ready for something more.

I approached my division manager about the possibility of

trading for Merrill. It proved to be the first time in my life that I came up against, and couldn't move, a barrier created solely by the fact that I was a woman. He was very definite—Merrill Lynch was years away from putting a woman on the floor of any of the exchanges, either as a trader or broker. It didn't matter that other firms had female brokers, or that my best friend was trading as a woman in the Corn Pit two floors away. It wasn't going to happen at Merrill Lynch anytime soon.

But he had an idea for me. There was a new product group at Merrill Lynch's Wall Street Headquarters, and if I was interested, he'd set up an interview for me. He told me he believed that the group and the account they were beginning to market, was about to become one of the company's most important financial products.

I agreed to interview, and landed the job with Merrill Lynch's national Cash Management Account team. My manager's instincts were right, CMA did turn out to be a product that changed the face of both brokerage and banking in the United States, and I was lucky to have been part of that.

But before I left Chicago for Manhattan at the end of June 1978, there was time for one more Lake Geneva memory. It was a ruckus croquette game and dinner that I hosted on the front lawn at Ceylon Point with my eclectic group of friends—a wonderful mix of summer people, locals from both Lake Geneva and Fontana, and one soon to be tourist. Me.

I can close my eyes and still see the late afternoon sunlight slanting across the lawn as we malleted our balls from hoop to hoop, cocktails at the ready. We were in our early twenties, beginning what would become our futures. In khakis and sleeveless summer dresses, we played barefooted on the cool green grass. The lake was a sparkling backdrop of light, and the view from the point down the lake to Fontana was nothing short of sublime.

I returned to the lake several times a year over the next five years for holidays, friends' weddings, and baby showers. When I got married in 1981, my parents held our reception at Ceylon Point. On a gorgeous July afternoon, they hoisted enormous tents on the broad lawn of the point overlooking the lake, and we danced and celebrated late into the night.

Eventually, my parents sold the house at Ceylon Point and moved to Palm Beach, Florida. Like me, my sisters and brother had all settled outside of the Midwest. Both our homes at Tanglewood and Ceylon Point still stand, though, to some degree or another, significantly changed by time and new, Lake Geneva-loving residents.

I spent six amazing years in New York. In due course, life would lead me to other jobs and cities, children, divorce, lots of travel, and many more adventures.

I raised my daughters on stories of Lake Geneva—of the water, the hundred-acre field, catching minnows and crayfish, sailing, water skiing, and, of course, becoming the Mail Girl. I wove wonderful tales for them, full of excitement, adventure, and magic. Every one of them true.

I have come to believe that the true essence of Lake Geneva is a little bit of magic. No matter what the era, the style, or the year; whether you spend your summers here, live here year-round, or visit for a weekend or a day; there is something that glimmers in the air above the lake—something that is as much felt as it is seen. It's the laughter of children chasing fire flies, the scent of the grill, the rush as the sail fills, the glittering reflection of the sun, the cool refreshment of the water against your skin.

And, at the end of the day, looking out across the lake from wherever you are and thinking: *Life is beautiful.*

Bibliography

Wikipedia—Arts and Crafts Movement. Accessed 2013. <http://en.wikipedia.org/wiki/Arts_and_Crafts_movement>.

Wikipedia—Chautauqua. Accessed 2013. <http://en.wikipedia.org/wiki/Chautauqua>.

Wisconsin Historical Society, Black Point Estate. Accessed 2013. <http://blackpointestate.wisconsinhistory.org>.

Town of Geneva Wisconsin. Accessed 2014. <http://www.townofgenevawi.com/about-the-town>.

City of Lake Geneva. Accessed 2013. <http://www.cityoflakegeneva.com>.

Wikipedia—Gilded Age. Accessed 2014. <http://en.wikipedia.org/wiki/Gilded_Age>.

Wikipedia—Great Chicago Fire. Accessed 2014. <http://en.wikipedia.org/wiki/Great_Chicago_Fire>.

Wikipedia—History of Chicago. Accessed 2014. <http://en.wikipedia.org/wiki/History_of_Chicago>.

Wikipedia—English Country House. Accessed 2013. <http://en.wikipedia.org/wiki/English_country_house>.

Wikipedia—Romanticism. Accessed 2013. <http://en.wikipedia.org/wiki/Romanticism>.

Wikipedia—Victorian America. Accessed 2013. <http://en.wikipedia.org/wiki/Victorian_America>.

Frohna, Anne Celano, ed. 2010. *Geneva Lake Reflections, More Stories from the Shore*. Wlliams Bay, Wisconsin: Nei-Turner Media Group.

Gazlo. Accessed 2013. <http://www.gazlo.com/marketplace/businesses/webster-house-historical-soc/features/6685>.

Gage Marine. Accessed 2014. <http://www.gagemarine.com>.

Baumbach, Emil A. III. 22 March 2014. *Personal Communication*.

CannonBall:HNP. Accessed 2013. <http://www.cnbhnp.com/about_history.html>.

Wikipedia—Howard Van Doren Shaw. Accessed 2013. <http://en.wikipedia.org/wiki/Howard_Van_Doren_Shaw>.

Boston Whaler. Accessed 2013. <www.bostonwhaler.com>.

Friestad, Harold. 10 September 2013. *"Personal Communication."*

"US Mail Boat Informational Sign." Riviera Pier, Lake Geneva, Wisconsin.

Gage, Mary Burns, and Wolfmeyer, Ann. 1976. *Lake Geneva, Newport of the West 1870 -1920, Volume I*. Lake Geneva, Wisconsin: Lake Geneva Historica Society, Inc.

Wikipedia—Lee Phillip Bell. Accessed 2013. <http://en.wikipedia.org/wiki/Lee_Phillip_Bell>.

M-20 Association. Accessed 2014. http://<www.m20-scow.com/history.html>.

Melges Boat Works. Accessed 2014. <http://www.melges.com/?p=pages/bio/buddy-melges>.

Funding Universe. Accessed 2013. <http://www.fundinguniverse.com/company-histories/swift-company-history>.

Globe Corporation. Accessed 2013. <http://www.globecor.com/about/history>.

Chicago Tribune. Accessed 2013. <http://articles.chicagotribune.com/1992-11-11/news/9204120107_1_mr-getz-lake-geneva-water-safety>.

Chicago Tribune. Accessed 2013. <http://articles.chicagotribune.com/1988-05-11/news/8803160086_1_morton-salt-morton-international-french-firm>.

Lake Geneva Estates. Accessed 2013. <http://www.lakegenevaestates.com/top-10-mansions-2/driehaus-estate>.

Wikipedia—Equal Rights Amendment. Accessed 2013. <http://en.wikipedia.org/wiki/Equal_Rights_Amendment>.

Wikipedia—Works Progress Administration. Accessed 2013. <http://en.wikipedia.org/wiki/Works_Progress_Administration>.

Sperry Top-sider. Accessed 2013. <http://www.sperrytopsider.com/en/content?caid=our-story>.

Haeger, Steve. 10 September 2013. *"Personal Communication."*

Friestad, Harold. 07 February 2014. *"Personal Communication."*

Lake Geneva Cruise Lines. Accessed 2013. <http://www.cruiselakegeneva.com/riviera.php>.

Encyclopedia of Chicago. Accessed 2013. <http://www.encyclopedia.chicagohistory.org/pages/2841.html.

Hobie Cat. Accessed 2013. <http://www.hobiecat.com/sail/hobie-16>.

Lake Geneva Water Safety Patrol. Accessed 2014. <http://watersafetypatrol.org>.

GenDisasters. Accessed 2013. <http://www.gendisasters.com/data1/wi/ships/lakegeneva-boataccjul1895.html>.

Wikipedia—Columbian Exposition. Accessed 2013. <http://en.wikipedia.org/wiki/World%27s_Columbian_Exposition>.

Los Angeles Times. Accessed 2013. <http://articles.latimes.com/1985-04-09/news/mn-28007_1_united-airlines>.

Pintrest. Accessed 2013. <http://www.pinterest.com/sparklenut/ceylon-court-fr-chandler-1900-jj-mitchell-1901-mag>.

Time Magazine. Accessed 2013. <http://content.time.com/time/magazine/article/0,9171,731207,00.html>.

Keefe, Michael. 22 March 2014. *"Personal Communication."*

CPSIA information can be obtained at www.ICGtesting.com
Printed in the USA
LVOW13s2059030714

392901LV00002B/3/P